T0334336

Cambridge Elements

Elements in Creativity and Imagination
edited by
Anna Abraham
University of Georgia, USA

OUTSIGHT

Restoring the Role of Objects in Creative Problem-Solving

Frédéric Vallée-Tourangeau
Kingston University

CAMBRIDGE
UNIVERSITY PRESS

Shaftesbury Road, Cambridge CB2 8EA, United Kingdom

One Liberty Plaza, 20th Floor, New York, NY 10006, USA

477 Williamstown Road, Port Melbourne, VIC 3207, Australia

314–321, 3rd Floor, Plot 3, Splendor Forum, Jasola District Centre, New Delhi – 110025, India

103 Penang Road, #05–06/07, Visioncrest Commercial, Singapore 238467

Cambridge University Press is part of Cambridge University Press & Assessment, a department of the University of Cambridge.

We share the University's mission to contribute to society through the pursuit of education, learning and research at the highest international levels of excellence.

www.cambridge.org
Information on this title: www.cambridge.org/9781009529730

DOI: 10.1017/9781009529693

First published 2024

A catalogue record for this publication is available from the British Library

ISBN 978-1-009-52973-0 Hardback
ISBN 978-1-009-52972-3 Paperback
ISSN 2752-3950 (online)
ISSN 2752-3942 (print)

Additional resources for this publication at www.cambridge.org/Vallee-Tourangeau

Outsight

Restoring the Role of Objects in Creative Problem-Solving

Elements in Creativity and Imagination

DOI: 10.1017/9781009529693
First published online: November 2024

Frédéric Vallée-Tourangeau
Kingston University
Author for correspondence: Frédéric Vallée-Tourangeau,
f.vallee-tourangeau@kingston.ac.uk

Abstract: The way we understand and treat creativity in psychology is currently built on a fundamental asymmetry between people and objects: people have thoughts, intentions, and the ability to act, while objects lack these qualities. However, despite this distinction, the objects that are created communicate with their creator, in a way. During the process of creating something, the objects being formed by the creator take on certain characteristics and behave in certain ways. This results in a kind of conversation between the person working on solving a problem and the results physically produced. In essence, while the traditional view focuses on the person's thoughts and intentions as the driving force of creativity, the dialogue between the creative individual and the evolving product of their work is overlooked. A methodology and a theoretical vocabulary that restore the role of objects in the dynamic unfolding of creative problem-solving are proposed. This title is also available as OpenAccess on Cambridge Core.

This Element also has a video abstract: www.cambridge.org/Vallee-Tourangeau

Keywords: creativity, problem-solving, insight, interactivity, dialogic cognition

ISBNs: 9781009529730 (HB), 9781009529723 (PB), 9781009529693 (OC)
ISSNs: 2752-3950 (online), 2752-3942 (print)

Contents

We are surrounded by creativity and are, generally, the better for it. For now, let's put aside definitions of creativity and efforts to distil creativity into essential, necessary features, such as value (Csikszentmihalyi, 2014), intentionality (Weisberg, 2015), or satisfaction (Abraham, 2023). Let's also bracket scalar or relative considerations, big or mini, personal, or historical. A child utters a surprisingly complex structure that pleases her and her parent; a graphic designer juxtaposes two images to arresting effect; a sculptor adopts a new way of working with clay after a protracted period of stagnated progress; a musician derives a new melody by exploring different note combinations; a writer uncovers a new felicitous structure through rewriting and editing her text; a researcher tweaks a laboratory preparation and unveils a new window onto a complex phenomenon; a software engineer changes a few lines of codes to satisfying effect; I could go on (and on). It's difficult to resist the urge to identify a common element to all these examples; if we can't, we could say without controversy that creativity is something new, a sentence, a sculpting gesture, a melody, a literary output, an experimental preparation, and so forth. New for whom is often how rhetorical reflections on creativity unfold, but that is not something that concerns me here, it's the novelty that does.

How new ideas come to people is what interests me. We can understand (and forgive) the intuition that the root of the process that evinces a new idea is cognitive in nature. It is eventually expressed in words, which reinforces the intuition that the new idea comes from a person and her cognitive ability to articulate it. In addition, histories identify a point in time when the new idea was expressed, ideas are given temporal coordinates, a before and an after, that encourages diachronic story telling of its genesis. And when the temporal transition is swift, we call it an 'insight' (Köhler, 1925). My contention, however, is that these intuitions feed narratives about the origin of new ideas that are, on the one hand, insufficiently granular and insufficiently developmental, and on the other hand, narratives that endow too much agency to an individual creator and hyperbolize her mind (and the cognitive processes herein; Vallée-Tourangeau, 2023b). This results in somewhat hagiographic accounts of creatives and their minds, in narratives of the type 'one day, so and so had an idea' (Latour & Woolgar, 1986, Chapter 4); in other words, that there is something special about the person or her mind, some kind of cognitive exceptionalism. There is a tautology lurking here: Creative people have creative ideas. It's a tautology that has encouraged generations of psychological researchers to identify so-called creative people – usually on the basis of tests of divergent or convergent thinking or scores on creative activity inventories – and then seek to identify what's exceptional about the structure of their semantic memory (e.g., Mednick, 1962; Benedek & Neubauer, 2013), their executive function processes (e.g., Zabelina et al., 2016), or other exceptional aspects of their associative learning abilities (such as latent inhibition, or lack of relative to less creative people; Carson et al., 2003). And if the cognitive exceptionalism is not endogenous, then efforts are made to produce it artificially through direct transcranial direct current stimulation to the right or left pre-frontal cortex (Li et al., 2023).

Insight and the Aha! Experience

For 'amusement', as he put it in his autobiography, Charles Darwin read Thomas Maltus's *Essay on the Principle of Population* on 28 September 1838. He connects a number of ideas in doing so: superfecundity, limited resources, death, survival, and selection. This idea bundle is one of the foundational principles of the origin of new species. What an insight! These connections flashed in his mind, according to Darwin (1958, p. 120): '(. . .) being well prepared to appreciate the struggle for existence which everywhere goes on from long-continued observation of the habits of animals and plants, *it had once struck me* that under these circumstances favourable variations would tend to be preserved, and unfavourable ones to be destroyed. The result of this would be the formation of new species' (my emphasis). Thus, a long period of preparation led to a sudden insightful connection of separate ideas, an aha moment if there ever was one. It remains curious, though, that in his notebook kept at the time (the D Notebook, Gruber & Barrett, 1974), Darwin mentions reading Malthus, but 'the crucial passage does not even contain a single exclamation point, although in other transported moments he used quite a few, sometimes in triplets. More significantly, he does not drop all other concerns and questions in a manner suggesting that he now feels he has the answer of answers to the "question of questions". The next day, September 29, we find a long entry on the behaviour of various primates, much of it about their sexual curiosity' (Gruber & Barrett, p. 170). Darwin's description of this insight was written 38 years later mind you (namely in 1876) and so we might question his recollection of how sudden it actually was, and the notebook entries at the time appear to underscore no specific affective experience of the aha type (see also Gilhooly, 2019, for critical reflections on retrospective accounts of sudden insights).

The terms 'insight' and the 'aha experience' enter the psychology of creative problem-solving in the early years of the twentieth century through the work of two German psychologists Wolfgang Köhler (Einsicht,[1] in his *Mentality of*

---

[1] From Vygotsky (1934/2012, p. 82): 'Köhler introduced the term insight (Einsicht) for the intellectual operations accessible to chimpanzees. The choice of term is not accidental. Gustav Kafka pointed out that *Köhler seems to mean by it primarily seeing in the literal sense* and only by extension "seeing" of relations generally, or comprehension as opposed to blind action'. (my emphasis).

the apes) and Karl Bühler respectively (*aha erlebnis*; Danek, 2023). Köhler working with chimpanzees, was keen to develop a non-associative account of problem-solving against a radical behaviourist backdrop. Vygotsky (1934/2012, p. 82) reproached Köhler's ambiguous use of the term: 'It must be said that Köhler never defines insight or spells out its theory. In the absence of theoretical interpretation, the term is somewhat ambiguous in its application: sometimes it denotes the specific characteristics of the operation itself, the structure of the chimpanzees 'actions; and sometimes it indicates the psychological process preceding and preparing these actions, an internal "plan of operations" as it were'. In turn, an aha moment is a multifaceted affective reaction experienced from the particularly pleasing connections between hitherto unrelated ideas. It isn't a process, but rather the outcome or product of the mental operations that established those connections as it comes to conscious awareness. Danek (2023, p. 313) writes:

> what exactly causes an Aha! experience: It is the emergence of a new association between formerly remote concepts or thoughts, when the thinker becomes aware of a new relation that can be made. The moment in which this new association becomes conscious is the fleeting moment of 'Aha!'. Importantly, this is not the moment when the association is formed, since the restructuring process happens earlier, but instead it is the moment when the final product of restructuring, the complete association, enters consciousness.

I will return to the notion of 'restructuring' and what the use of the term seeks to achieve shortly.

Insight as a Process. In Wiley and Danek (2024), we find a state-of-the-art statement on insight, wonderfully illustrated with their Figure 1 (p. 45). The temporal trajectory is segmented in terms of Wallas's (1926) five stages: preparation, incubation, intimation, illumination, and verification. Upon encountering a problem, the reasoner's interpretation guides her work (preparation). If the problem resists a solution at this stage, the reasoner experiences an impasse. Letting go of the problem, moving on to other things, her interpretation of the problem and its unsuccessful resolution stew at the back of her mind, unconscious (and uncontrolled) associations may form among different elements of her interpretation, as she consciously engages in other activities (incubation). These unconscious associations may configure a new interpretation of the problem, teasing her with the outline of a solution (intimation), which may result in an *insight*,[2] a full-blown aha moment (illumination). She then proceeds to implement the solution, establishing that her new

---

[2] 'the appearance of a complete solution with reference to the whole lay-out of the field' (Köhler, 1925, p. 190).

interpretation does unlock the solution to the problem (verification). Insight is fascinating because it marks a transition, from being stuck, that is from not knowing how to solve a problem, to one where the solution becomes glaringly obvious, and the problem solver marvels at her previous ineptitude. In retrospect, the solution appears obvious, and the reasoner may no longer appreciate or understand why she was so stuck, so stumped (Ohlsson, 1992).

Insight as a Procedure. To mobilize this phenomenon under laboratory conditions, researchers have developed an insight procedure. The procedure does not guarantee that problem-solving necessarily proceeds through this 'pure' insight sequence (as described in Wiley & Danek, 2024, and others, e.g., Fleck & Weisberg, 2013; Ohlsson, 1992), but it sets the stage for its occurrence. Participants are presented with simple problems, their appearance and the interpretation they encourage, lure participants to engage in a problem-solving strategy that leads them to an impasse. For example, participants read: 'Imagine a drawer with brown and black socks in a 4:5 ratio, how many socks must be drawn to obtain a matching pair?' Or: 'How to do you place 17 animals in four enclosures such that there is an odd number of animals in each enclosure?' In the first, the ratio information is misleading, since with only two colours, drawing three would guarantee a match. In the second, the problem masquerades as a simple division problem, but seventeen cannot be split into four odd numbers: It's the spatial arrangements of the enclosure that permits a solution (by double counting animals in overlaps). There are many different types of insight problems – see Weisberg's (1995) taxonomy – some are verbal riddles the solution of which hinges on the reinterpretation of its meaning (how can a woman marry ten men in a year without breaking polygamous laws; on verbal stumpers see Bar-Hillel, 2021; Ross & Vallée-Tourangeau, 2022a), some involve simple arithmetic reflections (as in the socks problem; Ross & Vallée-Tourangeau, 2021b), or simple arithmetic skills with some visuo-spatial imagination (as with the seventeen animals; Vallée-Tourangeau et al., 2016). The gap between not knowing the solution and discovering it, the epistemic gap as it were, is in some sense 'unmerited' (Ohlson, 1992, p. 4) because the knowledge and reasoning or numeracy skills required to solve the problem are well-within the skill set of the participants.

The insight procedure thus simulates creative problem-solving in that the reasoner has to abandon the original unproductive interpretation of the problem – and the concomitant method to solve it – and discover a new interpretation that cues a new method to the solution. In other words, the procedure offers a window onto the genesis of a new idea (I will return to how clear the view from that window really is, though, below). The insight problem is designed to create an impasse and the breakthrough can only be achieved through conjuring a new idea. The researcher is thus poised to capture this moment and interrogate the process through which this idea is produced.

Totus in Mente. We commonly encounter the term 'restructuring' in insight problem-solving research: The new idea is the result of a restructured interpretation of the problem, one that brings the solution within the reasoner's mental look ahead horizon (Ohlsson, 1984). Vygotsky (1934/2012, pp. 216–217) offers this description: 'The problem X that is a subject of our thought must be transferred from the structure A within which it was first apprehended to the entirely different context of structure B, in which alone X could be solved'. It is eminently plausible to cast restructuring in cognitive terms. Models of insight problem-solving – as illustrated in Wiley and Danek (2024) – have at their starting point a mental representation of the problem: It is an interpretation of the problem and a mental simulation of how these elements could coalesce to form a solution. If the reasoner experiences a breakthrough, one points to a change in the mental representation of the problem. What explains this change in mental representation? Here, theorizing efforts meet a fork in the road. One path leads to a deliberate (quasi) systematic inspection of the separate elements of the problem representation that labour a new set of relations among these elements. This type of explanation, drawing as it does on conscious effortful analysis, is what has come to be labelled 'business as usual' (see Vallée-Tourangeau, 2023a for a brief review): There is nothing special about the cognitive processes implicated in insight problem-solving, it's the same kind of processes that are involved in, say, mental arithmetic, drawing on working memory resources and knowledge of operators that transform and combine separate elements into a solution.

The other path from the fork points to an explanation where conscious analysis plays a secondary role. Rather, the initial mental representation is built from certain patterns of activation in semantic memory. The elements of this semantic network may themselves activate adjacent concepts, which may trace new paths in semantic memory. Thus, reverberations from the initial mental representation, too subtle to rise to consciousness initially, may connect new elements in semantic memory that may coalesce in a new mental representation of the problem (a difficulty with accounts that bank on unconscious processes is how to explain the transition to consciousness). Thus, the reasoner's mind may conjure up, during a so-called period of incubation, a new representation that brings the solution within a *mental* look ahead horizon. The term 'incubation' is also interesting: An incubator protects an organism from the outside world, seals its development to prevent external factors from interfering with it. Incubation may result in a solution by way of a period of doing something else (e.g., Gilhooly et al., 2013), withdrawing from the problem, letting ideas simmer unconsciously.

Which of these two paths offer a better route to explain the nature of the solution process with insight problems is a question that has animated many researchers over the past 25 years. The choice is made difficult for two reasons. First, classifying a problem as belonging to the insight kind does not guarantee that it will be solved with insight (Bowden & Grunewald, 2018): A participant may solve such a problem without experiencing an impasse and in the absence of the sudden restructuring of a mental representation. This unpredictability is compounded by a research strategy that measures performance aggregated over sets of insight and non-insight problems (e.g., Gilhooly & Fioratou, 2009; Gilhooly & Webb, 2018). These aggregate measures are then correlated with measures of working memory capacity and executive functions. Positive correlations between working memory and insight problem-solving performance are interpreted as undermining special processes and lending support to a business-as-usual process, that is, a process that draws heavily on conscious deliberate analysis of the problem (Chuderski & Jastrzębski, 2018). But if an insight problem might not set the stage for a pure insight sequence (of the type illustrated in Wiley & Danek, 2024) and if how an *individual* participant solves a *specific* problem can't be recovered from aggregate indices of performance, then such correlational evidence is impossible to interpret and, in any case, probably meaningless. A much more granular qualitative analysis of problem-solving is required to illustrate different solution processes, as I will demonstrate below. But for now, the point I wish to make is not whether one account is better suited than the other. Both accounts share something in common: whether conscious or unconscious, problem-solving proceeds with mental representations that are restructured through cognitive processes. It's all in the mind.

Taking Creativity Out of the Mind: Lessons from Objects

Buchman (2021) prefaces his book, *Make to Know*, with an interview with Tim Kobe, CEO of the design firm Eight Inc. Kobe and his teams, in collaboration with Steve Jobs, designed the Apple Store, a retail concept that marked a radical departure from the 'stack it high, let it fly' design of so many retail surfaces (then and now). Open space, large Parsons tables sparsely populated with Apple products, surfaces that enhance the devices' interactive affordances, lighting, materials (glass, wood), the spatial arrangement of all these elements (including the Genius Bar) curated a unique retail environment and singular shopping experience. The store embodied Apple's vision of 'making technology human' (p. 14). But vision alone is not sufficient for the physical realization of the store. The design process is one of iterative physical prototyping and discovery: the store came to be through making rather than simply thinking. Kobe says:

We started with bubble diagrams for the store, just saying 'let's try this or look at that'. We then went from sketches and drawings to small physical models. We were making a physical model each week of different things. And then we went to full-size models in a mock-up room. We produced some component of the store every week in foam-core mock ups. [Jobs] would walk around the models and look at them, fully realized in space. It all evolved until *we found what felt like Apple*. Along the way we found a lot that didn't work, that was too self-conscious, too technical, etc. When it didn't work, we would just tear the models down, or move them around, rebuild them, adjust things. (Buchman, p. 12, my emphasis)

Rather than simply reflecting the implementation of an idea, the retail space was *discovered* through physical prototyping. And before the first Apple store was built and opened to the public (May 2001), Apple rented a warehouse and built a full-scale prototype 'to explore ideas and test concepts . . . Jobs' appreciation of the iterative process of making became glaringly evident' (Kobe quoted in Buchman, p. 15; see also Ken Kocienda's (2018) *Creative Selection* for the description of a similar iterative process in the creation of the first iPhone).

Innovative design is a reflective practice (Schön, 1982), a dialogic process involving objects – for example, sketches and maquettes – that can be interrogated, that offer feedback, cue actions, seed new ideas. This dynamic and contingent interaction between designer and prototype 'means that there is no direct path between the designer's intention and the outcome' (Schön & Bennett, 1996, p. 175). Hartmann et al. (2006, p. 299) write: 'Prototyping is the pivotal activity that structures innovation, collaboration, and creativity in design'. Innovation proceeds by '*working it through*, rather than just *thinking it through*' (p. 299). Prototypes provide 'backtalk' (Böhmer et al., 2017) that 'helps designers discover problems or generate suggestions for new designs' (p. 956). Vandevelde et al. (2002) outline the many ways in which physical prototyping enhances the design process: prototypes are a source of new ideas, foster discovery, enhance efficiency (by identifying flaws early in the product development trajectory), facilitate communication in collaborative design environments (one is reminded of Star and Griesemer's (1989) boundary objects[3]), focus attention, and mark a project's developmental milestones, among many

---

[3] In any detailed description of the creation of a complex organization, boundary objects represent a class of heterogenous artefacts that link and articulate the interests and concerns of an equally heterogenous group of stakeholders and participants. Star and Griesemer introduced the concept in their analysis and description of the collaboration, interaction, and integration of such a group of heterogenous participants – botanists, zoologists, investors, collectors, trappers, university administrators – in the creation of The University of California's Museum of Vertebrate Zoology at Berkeley. Star and Griesemer sought to understand what objects could offer a platform that brought these people together, articulating their varied interests and preoccupations into a shareable representation. As Oswick and Robertson (2009, p. 180) write: boundary objects

others. Thus, creativity manifest in the design process, is scaffolded by physical prototyping unfolding over time, space, and in collaborative design, people. An innovative product is *discovered*, not through mental manipulation and representational restructuring, but through making things, and interrogating how these things look and behave. As Schrage (1999, p. 77) puts it, prototypes are partners in thinking, they are 'provocative', raising 'questions that have never been asked before'; they 'create new realities' (p. 54). Clearly, there are ideas that initiate prototype construction, but these are transformed by the process of making as well as by observing the result of the constructed prototype. Mental restructuring, so fondly conjured up by insight researchers, may well ensue, but a change in a mental representation may *follow* rather than precede the physical restructuring of the object qua prototype.

Respecifying Creativity. Science and technology studies along with ethnomethodology offer a rich source of case studies on creativity and innovation, and in the process aim to 'respecify' creativity (part of a larger project on respecifying cognition, see, e.g., Coulter, 1991). Most are historical analyses (e.g., Bryant's (1976) treatment of the Diesel engine; Latour's (1999) analysis of Joliot's discovery of nuclear fission) but many are based on in situ ethnographies (see Lynch & Woolgar, 1990). These case studies proceed by heeding, implicitly or explicitly, Latour's (1987) seventh rule of method outlined at the end of his *Science in action*, namely a moratorium on cognitive explanation of science and technology. Latour is not advocating an old-fashioned form of radical behaviourism, far from it. Of course, people have ideas and mental representations. The question is whether these ideas *explain* the chain that threads the contingent experimental manipulations or engineering tinkering that eventuate in discoveries, or are constituted by practice, here actions upon, and interactions with, things. If the latter, then we must look at how human actors interact with a broad range of heterogenous elements, objects and technological artefacts that configure a physical environment within and through which thinking is done. His seventh rule of method simply states that before resorting to cognitive exceptionalism to explain an innovation, we should first proceed with a thick granular description of the interactions that take place within this system. The complex interactions among people, and between people and things, underscore the distributed, extended and hybrid nature of cognition.

'are inscribed artefacts that in some shape or form capture, codify and/or represent some other, often tangible, object(s) to facilitate interaction across different social worlds [or stakeholders]'. Michael Schrage (1999) in his book *Serious play*, casts prototypes and models as playing similar roles. For example, quoting an Intel research manager, 'the use of informal demonstrations [of a prototype] facilitates communication between many people' (p. 29). A prototype offers a'"shared space" where ideas are created and their practical value debated' (p. 47). A prototype is a physical object that bridges disciplinary boundaries (among the different factions/departments of an organization); prototyping is 'a medium for interdepartmental integration' (p. 90).

The cognitive ecosystem (to use Hutchins's (2010) term) within which new ideas emerge forces us to adopt a *principle of symmetry* (Latour, 2005), one that treats human and non-human actants equally. What is a non-human actant? It could be anything (and that is the important and humbling reflection for cognitive psychologists): a draft report, a sketch, a maquette, a technological device, a financial model on a spreadsheet, a map, a foam mock-up, a software demo, a gesso primed canvas and so on. Following Latour (e.g., 1988), the word 'actant' is borrowed from semiotic and does not in itself attribute agency, insidiously, to non-human things (the ontology here is neutral, or perhaps agnostic). But the nature of these non-human objects and their 'behaviour', that is what they do or how they react to physical stimulations, have agentic consequences for their users, hence they are actants in the cognitive ecosystem.

Latour (2013, Chapter 6) reflects on three features of the developmental trajectory of a creative project (a sculpture in this instance). First, an object is created and made to do something (what Latour calls *faire faire*). This object, in the early phases of this trajectory is far from the finished product, it's an initial lump of clay shaped with gestures or tools. Second, the result can be evaluated in terms of its quality or defects, its shape unveils a dynamic field of affordances which guide the sculptor's next movements that will transform it into yet another intermediate object, and this iterative cycle of construction-evaluation-construction maps the route to the completion of the project. Third, agency is problematized in an interesting manner. To be sure, attributing agency makes sense for certain things, but not others: we may say that a sculptor has agency and uncontroversially that clay doesn't. Yet, the sculptor's agency is guided and constrained by the type of clay, its humidity, presence of fibrous additives, etc., as well as the malleability and structural properties of the evolving structure. How clay and the structure behave has agentic consequences for the human who sculpts it (March, 2024). Thus, agency is distributed, it is something that is enacted as a function of a system composed of different actants – to use semiotic terminology – some human, others non-human.

Interactivity and Insight Problem-Solving

In his famous monograph, Duncker (1945, p. 71) speaks of 'the importance of varied commerce with things and situations for problem solving'.[4] With 'commerce', Duncker forefronts the importance of interacting with objects. Yet, how psychologists typically investigate creative problem-solving has largely ignored

---

[4] Duncker coined this phrase following the description of a simple observational study with eight infants (8.5–13.5 months old; pp. 69–70): an attractive object is placed on a table out of reach, along with a stick that is within reach. Playing with the stick for half of these infants evolved into using the stick as a tool, which was used to bring the desirable objects within reach. Duncker (p. 70) writes: '*As a rule, use of the stick as a tool arises from playful commerce with the stick*

Duncker's observation.[5] The procedure commonly employed can be called 'second order' (Vallée-Tourangeau & March, 2020). It is second order because it plays out on an abstract conceptual plane, and as a result can only test certain explanations of problem-solving as manifest on that plane (a methodology makes visible certain phenomena, and *other* others (Law, 2004); it is performative in this respect).

Consider the innovative design and use of matchstick arithmetic problems reported in Knoblich et al.'s (1999) influential paper. Here, a simple, but false, arithmetic expression with Roman numerals is presented to participants, for example I = II + II but with sticks of the same length and width used to express operands and operators as illustrated in Figure 1. The task is to turn the expression true by moving one matchstick; not to remove a matchstick, but rather to move one stick from one operand or operator to another operand or operator to produce a true arithmetic expression. This is a Type B problem (as defined by Knoblich et al.) of relative difficulty: it involves relaxing the operator constraint, that is participants are likely to first seek to transform an operand, but the solution here involves discovering that it's through deconstructing the plus into a minus and moving the freed vertical stick from the plus to the operand on the left, creating a new operator and a new operand: I = III − II.

For all the action affordances of matchsticks (touching, lifting, moving, etc.), the procedure employed by Knoblich et al. actualize none since here participants are presented with the false equations on a computer monitor as a static image: participants stare at the screen for up to 5 minutes and either manage to announce a solution or not. Participants must perforce mentally simulate movement and transformations to arrive at an answer. There is no 'commerce with

Figure 1 A matchstick arithmetic problem. A false expression can be turned into a true one by moving a single stick to create a new operand or operator, or in this instance, both.

---

and – by way of the stick – with the object. An approach of the object which accidentally occurs in this situation leads to the discovery that the stick-toy is suitable as a tool' (italics in the original).
[5] Take for example the studies listed in Tables 1 and 2 of the Wiley and Danek's (2024) review. These tables identify twenty-six insight problem experiments; *none* of them employ a procedure that invites participants to interact with artefacts while engaging with the problem-solving task. This is not to say that insight problem-solving researchers never employ interactive tasks; I will review some of these interactive studies in the final section of this Element.

things', no dynamic interaction with objects; rather the solution process can only manifest as a cognitive operation on a mental representation.

A first-order insight procedure, in contrast to a second-order one, employs the same material, here illustrated with matchstick arithmetic problems, but where participants can manipulate the elements that configure the problem, testing new models of the solution by looking at them, rather than through mental simulation (Weller et al., 2011). This is first order because participants think with and through the world. It doesn't mean that more abstract thinking is excluded, certainly participants formulate hypotheses and can mentally simulate movements before physically constructing or implementing the mental simulation. But a first-order procedure changes 'the terrain of cognition', as Kirsh (2010, p. 442) would say. Cognition is augmented and transformed, interactivity couples mental processes with physical processes, offering an opportunity for a more symmetric collaboration between the two.

Interacting with physical objects, for example matchsticks that configure a model of the solution, puts objects on centre stage: The model's dynamic morphology is as important to the problem solver in her process of discovery, as it is to the psychological researcher for her goal to understand it. For now, let's cast aside the question as to whether actions that change objects and transformed the model of the solution were premeditated with a specific hypothesis, a hazy hunch, or simply reflects an unpremeditated playful interaction. Instead, let's focus on the information that a physical change in the model provides. Figure 2 shows three matchstick arithmetic problems: II = III + I, I = II + II, III = II − I. Panel A illustrates changes that result in models that depart from the correct model of the solution (namely, II = II + II, II = II + I, II = II − II). While these are not good models, the models are not devoid of information in that they

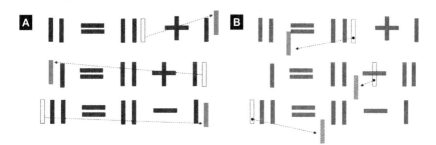

Figure 2 Matchstick movement: The transparent stick is the starting position, the light blue stick is the space where stick movement ends. Panel A illustrates how some movements produce new object-models of the solution that are far removed from the solution; Panel B illustrates how new objects approximate more closely the solution.

help participants appreciate that the solution cannot be created in this manner (it's the type of negative feedback guidance that physical prototyping can provide, helping designers cast aside certain ideas). Panel B illustrates movements that results in much more promising configurations, objects that approximate or create the solution (namely, III = II + I, I = III − II, II = III − I). This positive information may reinforce the movement, enacting the solution right before the participants' eyes. The solution is discovered through the creation of new objects.

As in physical prototyping in design, prototypes can be inspected and interrogated; the prototypes carry information that guides actions and cue new ideas. From the perspective of the researcher, objects and their transformation can be traced developmentally. They are data that help the researcher map the route along which a new idea was discovered. This process of discovery is exposed through the model's intermediate forms, just as the genesis of a work of art can be understood through a granular analysis of its different stages of production (Vallée-Tourangeau, 2023b, Chapter 6). The artwork was preceded by rich ideas and reflections as to what it could achieve to be sure, in addition to the conceptual narrative that can be retrospectively fitted by the artist and the gallerist in equal measure. However, the granular analysis of its production across time and space reveals a much more contingent and dialogic process with intermediate forms that becomes invisible in the finished product. A first-order insight procedure lays the ground for a detailed qualitative capture of the changes to the objects, in the case of matchstick arithmetic, proto models of the solution, and these material traces map out the route along which a new idea, in this case the solution to the problem, was constructed.

To sum up, a first-order insight procedure invites participants to construct a model of the solution (see Vallée-Tourangeau et al., 2016; Vallée-Tourangeau et al., 2020; Ross & Vallée-Tourangeau, 2022b). These objects are solution prototypes, some promising, others less so. Still, these objects convey information in the same way that physical prototypes guide designers and artists. The dialogue with physical models is also at the heart of scientific discovery, as Watson's (1968, Chapter 26) discovery of the structure of DNA through the manipulation of cardboard models of base pairs illustrates (see Toon, 2011, on the importance of 'playing' with models of molecules). The restructuring process that is evinced through this interaction may not be mental in this respect, rather it may first be anchored in a physical change that then dictates a change in the mental representation of the problem. This has important implications for the psychology of creative problem-solving, one that forefronts the role of the objects and the dialogue they encourage and permit in the process of discovery (see also Trasmundi & Steffensen (2024) for a more general discussion of dialogic cognition).

A Methodological Proposal and Illustration

My interest is in the process of discovery in creative problem-solving. Using an insight procedure, my aim is to capture the moment the idea that unlocks the solution occurs. Aggregate measures of performance from a set of insight problems hide rather than reveal the process. Hence, the methodology should be more granular, one that helps trace the trajectory of discovery for one problem. The methodology should provide rich qualitative data. On the importance of physical prototyping, the procedure should permit interaction with artefacts through which participants can build models of the solution. This interaction and the models created along the way should be recorded; the ensuing dialogue should too.

I will illustrate what this methodological proposition offers with a simple insight problem-solving experiment that employs matchstick arithmetic problems. Participants are invited to solve three problems (and do so in the same order) each for a 5-minute period: II = III + I, I = II + II, III = II − I. Participants from a small opportunity sample ($N = 56$) were randomly allocated to one of two conditions: in one, a first-order procedure was employed where participants could manipulate the sticks to create models of the solution, and in the other, a second-order procedure where they could not change the physical appearance of the problem as it was presented, nor could they use gesture to anchor mental projections of movements. While I expected performance, in terms of solution rates and solution latencies to be better in the interactive (first order) condition (as in Weller et al., 2011), this was not the primary focus of this exploratory experiment (see the Appendix for a summary of the results in terms of solution rates and latencies in the two conditions). Participants were also tasked with verbalizing their thoughts as they worked on the problems. I used Perkins's (1981) verbal protocol instructions, and participants in both conditions first practiced speaking while thinking with a simple word search puzzle (see the Appendix for a more detailed description of the experimental procedure).

The procedure was initially designed during the pandemic lockdowns: Participants were run individually, and the testing session took place on Zoom (see Archibald et al., (2019) on the suitability of Zoom for qualitative research). At the start of the session, participants were emailed a deck of PowerPoint slides which they opened in edit mode. The task instructions, practice word puzzle, and matchstick problems were presented on these slides. Participants shared their screen and the experimenter[6] recorded the session. Using the PowerPoint drawing tools, participants completed the word search puzzle while articulating

---

[6] My thanks to Anna Green who conducted all test sessions. She also transcribed all videos and coded changes in the objects (in the interactive condition) using ELAN.

their strategies and getting accustomed to being prompted to do so if they were silent for more than five seconds. Following the completion of this verbal protocol practice, the matchstick arithmetic problems were introduced. Each of the three problems was presented on a grid, with labelled rows and columns (see Figure 3). Thus, the procedure was instrumentalized to permit the precise coding of the movement of a stick in the interactive condition. Participants in both conditions worked on each problem for up to 5 minutes. The video recording thus showed the PowerPoint slide on which the problem was displayed and captured the participants' verbal protocol as well as the movement of the sticks in the interactive condition. The video recording of the entire test session was edited into three shorter videos, one for each of the three problems. Each of these shorter videos were coded using ELAN (https://archive.mpi.nl/tla/elan; Max Planck Institute for Psycholinguistics, The Language Archive, Nijmegen, The Netherlands; see also Wittenburg et al., 2006).

ELAN offers a platform to code the timing of events in a video record with great granularity. In the control condition, two sets of annotations (or tiers) were developed (see, e.g., Figure 4a) capturing (i) the participant's utterances and (ii) the experimenter's utterances. In the interactive condition (see Figure 4b) two additional sets of annotations were possible namely (iii) whether a stick was moved and (iv) the resulting appearance of the arithmetic expression qua (proto) model of the solution. Thus, in the interactive conditions, the temporal juxtaposition of two data streams, namely the participant's utterances and the

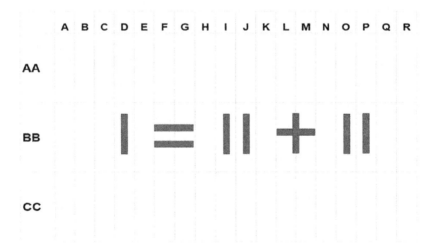

Figure 3 The matchstick arithmetic problems were presented on a grid with labelled rows and columns. The procedure was thus instrumentalized to permit the precise coding of the movements of each individual stick and the resulting model of the solution from the video recording of the session.

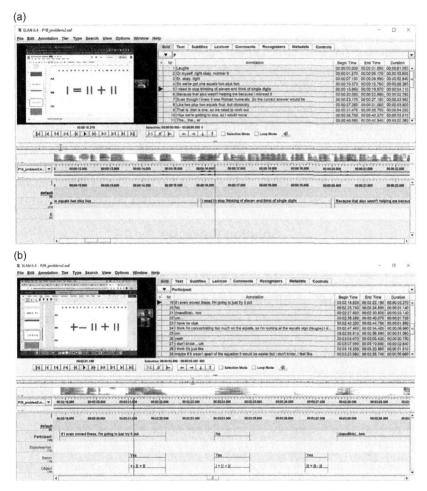

Figure 4 Screenshots of the annotations (or tiers) constructed in ELAN. In the control condition (a), the video was coded with two sets of annotations, corresponding to the participant's and the experimenter's utterances. In the interactive condition (b), two additional sets of annotations were constructed, namely whether a matchstick was moved and the resulting configuration of the arithmetic expression.

movement of matchsticks (and the resulting configuration of the equation) allowed the precise capture of whether a stick movement (and its consequence) was motivated by a hypothesis or strategy as well as how the participant reacted to the change in appearance of the arithmetic expression. This coding procedure maps the morphological change of the object qua model of the solution over time, as well as its role in guiding action and cueing new ideas. Two distinct solution processes could be clearly identified in the video evidence from the control condition, namely analytic and insight. The significant contribution of an interactive procedure is that it can make manifest a third yet unexplored phenomenon, one that can be termed 'outsight' (Vallée-Tourangeau & March, 2020; see also Steffensen et al., 2016; Vallée-Tourangeau et al., 2016). Outsight is object dependent; that is, the behaviour of the object reveals the solution. The participant's actions transform the object, but these transformations have uncertain outcomes, or at least, the participant does not anticipate the outcome of certain object-changes and only realises them once they are reified in the object. What follows is a description of the criteria employed to code the solution processes as well as transcripts along with links to the video evidence (on the OSF: https://osf.io/easb7/?view_only=6a69de18d3cd4c81ab9a824b26c7ac11).

Solution Processes

The process by which a solution was produced on successful trials within the allocated 5-minute period was determined on the basis of the verbal protocol data and video evidence. All videos were screened and coded independently by myself and a research assistant[7]; we then met to compare and discuss their classification and resolve disagreements. Three types of solution process were identified: Insight, analysis and outsight, the latter split into two sub-categories, post hoc and enacted.

Analysis. A solution process was deemed analytic when the participants clearly articulated a strategy or hypothesis that guided their exploration of the problem. It's not simply the articulation of the hypothesis that mattered here, but that the hypothesis was directly linked to the solution. In other words, the solution evinced through this process was the direct consequence of this exploration. The verbal protocol data indicate the conscious and deliberate consideration of possible movements, out of which the solution was derived. While the participants may express some joy and relief when their solution is confirmed as correct, there is no distinct aha! phenomenology that accompanies or shortly follows the announcement of the solution.

A transcript[8] from a participant in the interactive condition that was coded as analysis is reported in Table 1 (the video can be accessed on the OSF). This participant is working on Problem 3 (III = II − I); from the start the participant proposes that the III left of the equal sign is too large (00:08:2 'the equals is bottom heavy') which guides her exploration (00:18:8 'So something from the three has to go to the other side). The participant's movement is then guided by

---

[7] I thank Eleanor Stocker for her diligent and patient coding of the solution processes in both interactive and control conditions.

[8] I thank Alicja Perdion for generating and formatting the transcripts from the ELAN videos.

Table 1 A solution process coded as analysis in the interactive condition (P11, Problem 3).

00:00.9	P	Okay, great. So this is two minus one equals three
00:08.2	P	So obviously the equals is bottom heavy, so I already know that the three is too big
00:18.8	P	So something from the three has to go to the other side
00:24.0	P	So my brain has kind of automatically kind of done that, er
00:31.4	P	Even if I moved one of these (hovers on three), so I could
00:37.6	P	I think, no, there's not two. Ok, so . . .
00:41.3	P	My first thought it to maybe make that into a plus
00:41.3	B	Stick move
00:41.3	O	$\|=\|+\|$
00:44.5	P	So then that's two plus one
00:47.1	P	But that is incorrect, so making that a plus doesn't work
00:51.0	B	Stick move
00:51.0	O	$\|\|=\|-\|$
00:52.9	P	So then if I go back to the original
00:55.5	P	Thing, so I've got two minus one, so what I would need to do
01:00.2	P	Is go
01:00.3	B	Stick move
01:00.3	O	$\|=\|\|-\|$
01:01.8	P	Three minus one and that equals two

Note: The time stamp in the first column shows minutes:seconds.deciseconds.
P = Participant, E = Experimenter, B = Baton (or Stick), O = Object or the resulting physical appearance of the equation.

this hypothesis, first creating $II = II + I$ (adding a vertical stick from the III to the minus); but that did not work. The equation is re-set, and the next movement, still guided by the same hypothesis creates the solution. Thus, the solution is a consequence of movements informed by a clear strategy.

A transcript from a participant in the control condition that was coded as analysis is presented in Table 2 (the video can be accessed on the OSF). From the onset of the problem presentation (Problem 2, $I = II + II$), the participant focuses on the plus operator (00:25:4 'I'm focused on that bloody plus sign again so I'm going to explore all options so it's out of my head'). By changing the plus into a minus, the participant contemplates where the freed vertical stick can be placed, first mentally constructing $I = II - III$, then constructing the true expression $I = III - II$. Note that the participant does not wait for the experimenter to confirm the solution is correct, she knows it is the answer (00:43:9). There is no distinct aha! phenomenology expressed or on display, this is very much a so-called 'business-as-usual' process of conscious deliberation that

Table 2 A solution process coded as analysis in the control condition
(P30, Problem 2).

00:05.0	E	No honestly keep it up, keep talking like that, it's good
00:04.6	E	Ok I will start the timer, actually delete that slide
00:09.1	E	The second problem is on the next one
00:11.9	P	Ok cool
00:13.9	E	Five minutes will start when you're ready, ok
00:18.3	P	One equals two plus two, that's obviously false, correct
00:25.4	P	I'm focused on that bloody plus sign again so I'm going to explore all options so it's out of my head
00:31.7	P	Um two minus two, if I move the middle of the plus sign other to there
00:39.0	P	Two minus three, oh the other way, three minus two equals one
00:43.9	P	Which is correct, so I'd move the middle of the plus sign into J so it would be three minus two equals one, final answer

Note: The time stamp in the first column shows minutes:seconds.deciseconds.
E = Experimenter, P = Participant.

results in the correct answer. Note how the participant exploits the lettered coding grid to communicate to the experimenter where the vertical stick from the plus operator should be moving (which is something that some participants in the control condition did, and something that was not anticipated in the development of the procedure for this experiment; although perhaps I should have in light of Kirsh's (2009) study that demonstrates how mental projection is facilitated by an external structure that anchors it).

Outsight. A solution was coded as outsight when it was triggered from the external configuration of the problem. The purer cases of outsight are observed when the participants do not articulate specific strategies. Rather they move a stick to explore the consequent transformation of the object that is the physical model of the solution. There are also cases where the playful engagement with the task is a little less random, guided by a hunch, that a numeral or operator may be the key to the solution. However, the verbal protocol data indicate that participants cannot predict the outcome of a particular stick movement until they see that the new object created corresponds to the solution. Thus, rather than mental restructuring preceding the physical restructuring of the solution, *it's the other way around*. We identified two types of outsight processes: post hoc and enacted. A post hoc outsight occurs when participants recognize they constructed the solution to the problem after having created it, not during (and, of course, not before). Table 3 illustrates a session that showcased a post hoc outsight solution process for Problem 3 (III = II – I). The participant says 'I'm

Table 3 A solution process coded as post hoc outsight in the interactive condition (P19, Problem 3).

00:01.1	E	And I'll start the timer again, the third problem is on the thirteenth slide
00:07.2	E	ok I'll start the timer
00:07.2	P	ok so three equals two minus one, um so
00:18.7	P	um, I feel like I need to start moving things around to really see how it works, so two equals
00:23.0	B	Stick move
00:23.0	O	$\| = \| - \|$
00:28.0	P	two minus two is obviously not right because it's zero, so again
00:29.2	B	Stick move
00:29.2	O	$\|\| = \| - |$
00:34.5	P	um four equals ... I can't move, oh was that the original, oh yeah, so three equals two
00:45.8	P	two minus one, so this currently equals one and I need to make it equal three, no
00:57.8	P	yeah or make this equals two, or change
01:08.3	E	play around
01:10.0	P	yeah I'll play around, er so
01:14.6	B	Stick move
01:14.6	O	$\| = \| - |$
01:15.0	P	three so ok so I need to, I'm getting a bit stuck, so
01:16.4	B	Stick move
01:16.4	O	$\|\| = \| - |$
01:21.1	P	I can't
01:21.5	B	Stick move
01:21.5	O	$\| = \|\| - |$
01:22.7	P	move any of these
01:24.2	P	ah
01:25.1	P	laughs
01:26.8	P	I think I've done it
01:28.0	P	so two equals three minus one, um, this time
01:34.3	P	I don't, I think I just moved things around, um, and
01:46.6	P	it worked (laughs)
01:49.5	E	Did you see the solution after you moved it?
01:52.7	P	I did see the solution after I moved it, yeah
01:55.3	E	and you said 'ah'. that was
01:57.8	P	(laughs)
01:58.7	E	it was clicking, ok (laughs)

Note: The time stamp in the first column shows minutes:seconds.deciseconds.
P = Participant, E = Experimenter, B = Baton (or stick), O = Object or the resulting physical appearance of the equation.

getting a bit stuck' (01:15.0). He proceeds to move a stick from the III left of the equal, but the movement is not guided by a strategy. At 01:21.5, the correct model of the solution is constructed. Three seconds elapse, the participant first says 'Ah', then a second later he laughs, realizing he had constructed the solution.

In turn, an enacted outsight is observed when the solution to the problem is announced during a stick movement. At the start of the movement the participant has either not articulated a specific hypothesis or is working on an unproductive one (one that cannot result in constructing the correct matchstick configuration). The ELAN interface is particularly useful here in identifying occurrences of outsight enacted in the movement. Table 4 illustrates such a case: Here the participant is working on Problem 3 (III = II − I). A stick from the III

Table 4 A solution process coded as enacted outsight in the interactive condition (P39, Problem 3).

00:01.8	P	let's go, ok again, I'm going to imagine that it's left to right as the other ways have been
00:11.0	P	er . . . so . . . although I could make, no, equals . . . ah
00:20.8	P	no I can only move one, ok I'm going to make it as if it's left to right for a second, um
00:27.7	P	this one I might have to move, sorry I have to get my brain to figure out what's going on, sorry for some reason this one looks more confusing to me
00:38.2	P	um . . .
00:39.7	E	play around
00:41.0	P	yeah I'll play around, ok
00:43.2	B	Yes (slowly dragging stick from the III to the left of the equal sign; the movement lasts seven seconds until 00:51.0)
00:43.2	O	‖ = ‖‖ − │
00:43.7	P	so that's 2
00:47.2	P	er, oh no, wait, I can move this here
00:52.5	P	is that right, three minus one equals two
00:57.2	E	yeah
00:58.2	P	yeah, yeah ok cool
01:00.8	E	well done, so that one it seemed to me like you kind of got it as you were moving
01:08.2	P	yeah that was definitely, I don't know why but for some reason my brain thought it was more confusing than it was
01:16.7	P	and that was definitely as I moved it, I was like ok that makes more sense
01:21.3	P	I don't know what it was about that one, I don't know if it's the minus

Table 4 (cont.)

01:25.7	P	because the other one was plus, something else was plus maybe
01:29.2	P	I don't know, the other two were plus weren't they?
01:34.4	E	yeah they were
01:36.4	P	maybe it was something to do with that, my brain sort of saw
01:41.0	P	loads of, like an equals and a minus, and it threw it off for a second
01:47.8	P	but yeah that one was definitely as I moved it, that makes sense
01:51.8	E	and did you have any kind of strategy in mind before you moved it, or was it a random movement?
01:57.5	P	that was definitely a random movement, that was just, move that across and see what happens
02:03.8	P	yeah, brain sort of clicked into gear as I got it there
03:19.6	P	first one, and it was completely random I just started moved them across the screen, hoping that
03:23.8	P	my brain would kick in, yeah, I don't know.

Note: The time stamp in the first column shows minutes:seconds.deciseconds.
P = Participant, E = Experimenter, B = Baton (or Stick), O = Object or the resulting physical appearance of the equation.

left of the equal sign is selected and the participant proceeds to drag it towards the right of the equal sign; the movement is very slow spanning 7 seconds (this is more clearly seen in the video placed on the OSF). It is during the movement, as the object's transformation is initiated, that the participant realizes what the solution is.

Insight. Analytic and outsight solution processes are, in some relative sense, easy to distinguish in the video data: Distinct strategic effort guided by a hypothesis for the former (instances that can be observed in both the inter-active and non-interactive control condition), non-strategic and sometimes playful movement that results in an object that cues the solution in the latter. And while outsight can most clearly manifest through an interactive procedure, I will discuss a few cases of outsight in the control condition below. What of insight? We used the insight classification as a *fourre tout* category that is for any solution process that did not meet our analytic or outsight criteria. We should stress that our insight classification does not commit us to a certain model of the cognitive processes that result in insight: they may or may not result from the sudden pleasing Gestalt completeness of the solution that flashes in consciousness (e.g., Gilhooly & Webb, 2018) wrought by an unconscious or at any rate unreportable cognitive mechanism. Four criteria guided our classification of insight: (i) sudden occurrence of a solution in the absence of a voiced hypothesis or strategy or (ii) the sudden solution is diametrically different or orthogonal to an immediately preceding voiced strategy (in the control condition) and/or voiced or enacted strategy revealed by movement (in the interactive condition); (iii) the insight classification is stronger if accompanied by phenomenological markers of aha!; and (iv) the solution is expressed before a movement is enacted or announced, that is the solution precedes any physical or articulated transformation of the object or immediately follows a clear phenomenological epiphany and the solution is announced or is quickly assembled (in the interactive condition).

A solution process classified as insight in the interactive condition is illustrated in Table 5. The participant is working on Problem 1, namely II = III + I. At

Table 5 A solution process coded as insight in the interactive condition (P31 Problem 1).

00:00.1	E	Go
00:02.9	P	(deletes slide)
00:13.4	E	what are you thinking?
00:14.6	P	oh sorry I'm not understanding, so I'm thinking this is two equals three plus one, um so I need to make it two equals three minus one
00:26.5	P	so I need to move that stick
00:28.1	B	Stick move
00:28.1	O	$\| = \|\| - \|$
00:30.0	E	you can't get rid of a stick, you've got to just relocate it
00:33.4	P	Oh!
00:35.0	P	um
00:36.9	P	ok let me put it back
00:39.8	P	I'll put it back, oh god now I can't put it back, I made a mistake sorry, um, I'm thinking about the fact that I thought that was really simple and now I can't do that
00:44.1	B	Stick move
00:44.1	O	$\| = \|\| + \|$
00:49.7	P	(laughs) um
00:57.8	P	(sighs)
00:59.2	E	where are you looking?
01:01.2	P	I'm trying to work out, um
01:05.7	P	I'm looking at the one over here and I'm trying to work out . . . I can only move one stick
01:22.0	P	What I'm thinking about at the moment is, I'm a bit self-conscious because I'm thinking that it's supposed to be simple and I don't see the solution

Table 5 (cont.)

01:28.8	P	I'm getting a bit anxious about the fact that it's supposed to be simple but I can't um, work it out, so what I just need to try and think about, not being
01:40.2	P	um, not being self-conscious about that, so I'm going to think about what the figure says, so it says two equals three plus
01:42.2	E	yeah
01:48.9	P	one, and I thought that I could just make that into a minus . . . um
01:56.5	P	if I move that so that it's . . . if I moved that stick
02:03.1	P	Oh so that it was over here it would be three minus one, which doesn't work, so three
02:11.4	P	two equals four minus one doesn't work
02:18.9	P	mmm, I was just thinking, if I could move that
02:27.8	P	over there it still doesn't work does it, it's three minus one doesn't work
02:28.0	B	Stick move
02:28.0	O	$\|\|\| = \|\|\| - \|$
02:31.0	B	Stick move
02:31.0	O	$\|\| = \|\|\| + \|$
02:35.9	P	so two
02:40.3	P	two minus
02:43.6	P	three
02:46.2	P	mmm
02:49.2	P	I'm really struggling to work out what to do with the puzzle, and I'm
02:59.1	P	not sure that I can
03:02.6	P	answer it
03:05.6	P	two equals two . . . two equals two
03:15.6	P	oh, you stupid woman! (shouts)
03:16.2	B	Stick move
03:16.2	O	$\|\|\| = \|\| + \|$
03:18.7	P	I just worked it out, three equals two plus one
03:22.4	P	oh my god, I can't, honestly I can't. Is that right?
03:27.9	P	three equals two plus one
03:34.5	E	yeah, yeah, it's good (laughs)
03:37.4	P	no it's not good it took me about 40 minutes
03:41.3	E	it made me jump your exclamation of joy (laughs)
03:46.1	E	I fell asleep before that, joking, talk me through how you got that
03:59.1	P	I started talking to myself about the numbers, so instead of just staring at it and feeling like oh my god I can't

Table 5 (cont.)

04:09.8	P	do it and I've been told this is really simple, I actually, I narrated my, I just read it out to myself and then it
04:20.7	P	It made um more sense, I could see then which one I needed to move um so I think I was spending too much time looking at the equals and the plus, rather than
04:32.0	P	just um
04:36.4	P	I think because it was also Roman numerals, lots of lines, and I think if it had been written
04:45.0	P	numerical, you know
04:47.3	E	but in the instructions, it's not, the answer's not simple, it's how it's false is simple
04:56.6	P	laughs
04:58.4	E	yeah it's how the answer is false is simple, you know that the Roman numerals are
05:06.2	E	but actually getting there isn't so don't worry
05:11.8	P	(laughs) I'm so embarrassed
05:14.5	E	did you get the answer before you moved it?
05:18.4	P	yes
05:19.9	E	er, did you visualise it before you got it?
05:23.0	P	yes
05:24.4	P	yes because I narrated it to myself and I was just saying three, it's like self-directed speech made it clearer to me
05:35.8	P	so because I was saying two
05:39.6	P	equals three plus one, obviously that doesn't make sense, but
05:44.5	P	but then I worked out that if I just move that one it would be three
05:48.7	P	which equals two plus one
05:50.6	E	yeah
05:51.4	P	but it was because I was telling myself, I was
06:00.1	P	I talked myself through it out loud, I was trying to do it in my mind
06:02.9	E	yeah
06:06.0	P	I couldn't do it, but when I actually spoke it, it became clearer
06:10.7	P	and then I saw it quite quickly and then felt a bit silly that I'd taken that long
06:16.1	E	so it was really sudden when you got it
06:18.8	P	yeah

Note: The time stamp in the first column shows minutes:seconds.deciseconds.
P = Participant, E = Experimenter, B = Baton (or Stick), O = Object or the resulting physical appearance of the equation.

first, she wants to transform the plus operator into a minus. The experimenter (00:30.0) reminds her that she cannot delete a stick but must move it somewhere else. The participant expresses some anxiety, feels that she should be solving this quickly, and is self-conscious about being stumped by what she believes she should be able to solve quickly ('I'm getting a bit anxious about the fact that it's supposed to be simple but I can't um, work it out, so what I just need to try and think about, not being' 01:28.8). Her strategy remains focused on changing the plus operator into a minus. Nearly 3 minutes into the session, she is stumped, the impasse makes her think she can't solve the problem ('I'm really struggling to work out what to do with the puzzle, and I'm not sure that I can answer it' 02:49.2). Fifteen seconds later, in the absence of movement and any articulated strategy, an emphatic aha! moment is experienced: 'Oh, you stupid woman' (03:15.6) she shouts and proceeds to move a stick from the III right of the equal sign onto the II to its left to create the solution, namely III = II + I.

A solution process coded as insight in the control condition is illustrated in Table 6. The participant is working on Problem 1 (II = III + I). The order of the

Table 6 A solution process coded as insight in the control condition (P20 Problem 1).

00:00.1	E	The first problem will be on the next slide and I'll time it for five minutes when you're ready
00:06.1	P	Okay I'll delete now
00:11.4	P	I instantly know that's wrong because the plus and equals sign are going the wrong way, so
00:22.7	P	I don't know what this involves, BODMAS or something, I don't know, so two ...
00:37.1	P	Oh my god, I think I'm terrible at maths, I can't even do this one
00:40.1	E	What are you thinking?
00:42.3	P	I don't know, I feel like you can't have the equals so early on, it needs to be the sum first
00:52.1	P	But you can only move the stick once, right? So I guess the formula could go backwards like that
00:54.6	E	Yeah
01:01.6	P	It's not algebra is it? Okay, the letters are just there to confuse you
01:04.8	E	No
01:10.1	P	Oh, so move that, two minus
01:24.9	E	What were you going to say?

Table 6 (cont.)

01:27.7	P	I'm so confused. I'm thinking if the formula does go from right to left
01:35.2	P	Then maybe change the addition symbol, if you move the
01:44.0	P	The stick between M and N to Q
01:49.6	P	Does that work?
01:52.6	E	Could you read out what the sum would be?
01:59.2	P	Two Roman numerals
02:02.2	P	Minus three
02:07.0	P	Minus three . . . Equals two. No, um
02:14.1	P	But, I don't, I suppose the plus can't be there
02:22.5	P	But you can only move one stick, oh! Wait, no
02:28.9	E	What were you thinking?
02:30.9	P	Maybe if you move the sum, the result
02:37.8	P	to Q or something
02:42.2	P	Maybe you could, no, Oh! Yeah, I think I got it, so move I to E
02:50.0	E	I see what you mean, can you say the sum to confirm it?
02:55.4	P	It would be one Roman numeral, plus two equals three
03:01.0	E	Okay, you have read it backwards, but it still would make sense
03:08.5	E	That's the solution, well done
03:11.3	P	Yes!
03:15.0	E	How did you get that solution?
03:18.8	P	I was quite confused by the fact that it's going from right to left, but I think
03:29.5	P	I started reading it from right to left, but maybe I was still thinking even that
03:35.6	P	The end result had to come more from the right
03:38.8	P	I suppose it was kind of
03:41.2	E	Why did you think that?
03:43.4	P	I think I'm just so programmed to look at formulas from left to right, so seeing it um
03:50.6	P	Reverse kind of threw me off, and I think I was looking for the end product to be, and I think I was quite hung up on the
03:57.4	P	The plus, maybe that needed to be changed
04:01.9	P	But it did not in the end
04:03.6	P	The answer lied within the results, so
04:09.3	E	Was there anything in particular that helped you get the solution?
04:18.7	E	Because you were fixating on the plus, why was that
04:25.4	P	I don't know, maybe because it didn't make sense to me
04:32.5	P	I don't know why I fixated on the plus, um
04:38.0	P	I suppose because maybe if I could change the plus

Table 6 (cont.)

04:44.2	P	I could end up with a smaller answer like two
04:48.0	P	When the numbers are all four, maybe I should have focused on the numbers and not what
04:53.7	P	I suppose it's kind of taking, like
04:56.3	P	You're not looking at the maths so much, but you're looking for
05:00.4	P	The design in front of you
05:03.8	P	What you can do with it

Note: The time stamp in the first column shows minutes:seconds.deciseconds. P = Participant, E = Experimenter.

equation is a source of confusion at the start (sum then followed by the operands and operator, rather than the more common reverse order), and the confusion triggers the BODMAS mnemonic acronym concerning the correct order of operations in arithmetic (*B*rackets, *O*rders, *D*ivision, *M*ultiplication, *A*ddition, *S*ubtraction). She's not even sure this is an arithmetic problem (01:01.6). Once some of that confusion dissipates, the focus is on the operator, aiming to turn the plus into a minus (01:35.2). She then focuses on moving a stick from the total (the sum; 02:30.9) but gives up. Then a sudden 'oh' (02:42.2): she describes the movement of a stick from the III on the right of the equal sign to the II on the left of it by using the grid coordinates to describe the movement (from I to E). The experimenter asks her to read the result, and the participant says 'It would be one Roman numeral, plus two equals three' (02:55.4), reading it from right to left (reversing the order that caused her much confusion). This is coded as insight because the solution offered came to the participant suddenly and the immediately preceding hypotheses (changing the operator, moving a stick from the sum) are diametrically different from the solution announced.

Frequencies of Solution Processes: Interactive Condition. The coded solution process frequencies for each of the three problems are reported in Table 7. Of the seventy-four solutions (across participants and problems), coders agreed for fifty-six, and initially disagreed for eighteen. Of the eighteen cases of disagreements nearly all of them (fifteen out of eighteen), were about whether the solution process indicated insight or analysis (seven) or outsight of the post hoc or enacted kind (eight). All disagreements were resolved through discussion (and reviewing the video evidence jointly).

For all three problems, outsight was the most frequent solution process: 39%, 75%, and 48% of the solutions were the result of outsight for Problems 1, 2, and 3, respectively. Analysis was the second most frequent solution process – 35% for Problem 1, 25% for Problem 2, 44% for Problem 3. The least frequent

Table 7 Solution frequencies, solution process frequencies (Freq. and Percentage) for the three problems in the interactive and control conditions.

| | Interactive | | | Control | | |
| | II = III + I | | | II = III + I | | |
	Freq.	**%**			**Freq.**	**%**
Solutions	23		Solutions	20		
A	8	35%	A	11	55%	
I	6	26%	I	9	45%	
O-Ph	4	17%	O-Ph	0	0%	
O-E	5	22%	O-E	0	0%	
	I = II + II			**I = II + II**		
Solutions	24		Solutions	13		
A	6	25%	A	12	92%	
I	0	0%	I	1	8%	
O-Ph	8	33%	O-Ph	0	0%	
O-E	10	42%	O-E	0	0%	
	III = II − I			**III = II − I**		
Solutions	27		Solutions	24		
A	12	44%	A	12	50%	
I	2	7%	I	10	42%	
O-Ph	8	30%	O-Ph	2	8%	
O-E	5	19%	O-E	0	0%	

Note: A = Analysis; I = Insight; O-Ph = Post hoc outsight; O-E = Enacted outsight.

solution process was insight: none were coded as insight for Problem 2, 7% were coded as insight for Problem 3, and 26% were coded as such for Problem 1. Overall, then, out of the seventy-four solutions, there were forty instances of outsight (54%), twenty-six instances of analysis (35%), and eight instances of insight (11%).

Frequencies of Solution Processes: Control Condition. Table 7 also reports the coding for the solution process for all three problems for the control participants. Of the fifty-seven solutions in the control condition, coders' classification aligned for forty-one, and initially disagreed for sixteen. Of these disagreements, nine were about whether the solution process could be coded as insight or analysis, and seven whether it was analysis or a form of outsight. The disagreement were resolved through discussion while both coders watch the video together. Across all three problems, analysis was the most common solution process (61 per cent), followed by insight (35 per cent), and with two cases (or 4 per cent) of post hoc outsight.

I did not anticipate witnessing cases of outsight in the control condition. Of course, language is also a thinking tool (the 'ultimate artefact' as Clark (1997) puts it). Table 8 is a transcript from a participant in the control condition whose solution process was coded as outsight. The participant is working on the third problem (III = II − I), and his initial strategy focuses on the minus, aiming to turn it into a plus. He first proposes III = I + I; then he mentally simulates II = II + I, that is mentally moving a stick from the III left of the equal to change the minus into a plus. He despairs: 'I don't know why I'm struggling with this' (01:44.9).

Table 8 A solution process coded as post hoc outsight in the control condition (P54 Problem 3).

00:00.1	E	Click and delete, this is not the problem, the next one
00:04.1	P	ok
00:05.3	E	last one
00:06.8	P	and this is another one of the Roman numerals?
00:09.2	E	yeah
00:10.4	P	ok
00:12.1	E	go
00:12.4	P	shall I start?
00:13.3	E	yeah
00:15.4	P	so two minus one equals three, so minus one is one, so what if I move the
00:27.2	P	one from the two then it's one plus one, which equals three, not right that equals two, um what if I did
00:39.1	P	if I change the three and do
00:45.2	P	two, I keep thinking that's eleven, it's two, Roman numerals, so if I change the three to a two, I need to make that something equals two
00:58.0	P	um, I've already got a two there, that won't be able to do anything (?) so that doesn't work, um
01:08.1	P	and if I change the three to a two and make it into a plus that'll be two plus one which is three, not possible, ok
01:19.3	P	and so what else can I do? one, let's see, one minus
01:31.6	P	two minus one, two minus one is one, two minus one … two minus two is zero
01:44.9	P	two plus one, I don't know why I'm struggling with this
01:56.2	P	change that three and let's not put it onto any numbers, let's go
02:04.4	P	two plus one equals three (laughs) that's not right, no that is right but I wouldn't have three, I'd have two
02:19.6	**P**	**maybe I have to move that three then, otherwise I'm ending up with two minus two, which is zero, or three minus one**

Table 8 (cont.)

02:34.6	**P**	**oh wait**
02:38.7	**P**	**three minus one, is that it? I have to move,**
02:42.7	**P**	**I have to change that three to**
02:46.9	**P**	**yes that's all I have to do, all I have to do is move EBB to**
02:51.0	**P**	**to LBB and then it's three minus one which equals two**
02:56.1	E	yeah
02:57.4	E	correct, correct (laughs)
03:00.7	P	that was really stressful
03:04.4	E	um, how did you get that solution?
03:11.6	P	um, I don't know, I just kept saying every possible solution until I got to the last possible one I think
03:19.4	P	had to just keep narrowing it down until there was nothing left
03:25.4	E	would you say it was kind of a sudden flash or kind of analytical and logical?
03:32.3	P	um, I would say it was more sudden, I wouldn't say there was much, I mean there was logic in that I had to keep ruling things out but I was kind of immediate in that I got a bit excited when I found out the response

Note: The time stamp in the first column shows minutes:seconds.deciseconds.
P = Participant, E = Experimenter. The outsight sequence in the transcript is emphasized in bold.

His strategy then is to mentally move a stick from the III left of the equal in a systematic manner. He first mentally places on the minus, something he's already done, yielding II = II + I (02:04.4). What's interesting about this move, and while it might be following a strategy, he cannot clearly anticipate or understand its implication; there is no understanding here and this explains why he mentally creates something he knows doesn't work. And in the absence of understanding, he then says 'maybe I have to move that three then, otherwise I'm ending up with two minus two, which is zero, or three minus one' (the utterance starts at 2:19.6 and ends at 2:30.7): at the end of this 11 seconds span he articulates the solution (namely III − I) but there's no realization that he's done so. Four seconds go by and then the penny dropped, possibly: 'oh wait' (02:34.6) followed by 'three minus one, is that it? I have to move' (02:38.7) and 'I have to change that three to' (02:34.6) and five seconds later he uses the coordinate grid to anchor the description of the solution (02:51.0). This is a post hoc outsight because while a strategy was employed, the consequences of the simulated movement were not predicted, and even once the mental simulation produced the correct configuration, the answer was not recognized immediately. This is then a case where the answer is verbally produced in the absence of understanding. It's upon reflecting on his own verbal output that he understood that he had produced the right answer (but not before).

Reflections and Conclusion

This exploratory experiment illustrated the contribution of a certain methodology and analysis strategy to a clearer understanding of the processes that result in the discovery of a new idea, a methodology that reveals the role that objects can play in creative problem-solving. Let's summarize the key features of this methodology. First, it employs a first-order insight procedure, one that permits interactivity, one that invites the construction and manipulation of a model of the solution. Here, virtual rather than physical matchsticks were employed, and the decision to do so was to permit the remote testing of participants. Yet, materiality and embodiment matter in thinking and creativity (Kimmel & Groth, 2024; Malafouris, 2020; March, 2024), and there will likely be interesting research avenues to explore how these factors shape creative problem-solving. However, my focus – and what the methodology here was designed to capture – is the change in the model solution and how the resulting prototyping guided the discovery of a new idea. A second-order insight procedure (as employed in the control condition here), one where participants think though a verbal riddle or static graphical representation, completely ignores – and can't measure – the role of objects and their transformation in creative ideation and the importance of prototyping in making new thoughts. To use a Michel Serres (1994) metaphor, it's a bit like trying to make sense of a game of rugby without factoring the movement of the ball. If given I = II + II, the vertical stick from the plus operator is moved, the transient object may look like I = II − II; the object offers an interesting cue, and the participant can then make the object behave in different ways, by placing the stick in different places II = II − II or indeed I = III − II. It's not interactivity qua movements in and of themselves that are important; interactivity is not a panacea, it is not a universal degreaser that invariably oils the cognitive cogs. Interactivity is important because it changes how the world looks, it constructs new objects, the appearance and behaviour of which can be interrogated. These new objects are not representations of ideas they are the manifestation of them. Should restructuring happen, it's not mental but physical: It's the physical presentation of the problem that is restructured and which leads to the recognition of the solution.

The second key feature of the methodology illustrated here is its focus on single problems, and the process that evinced a solution. Aggregating performance on a set of insight problems hides rather than reveals the actual solution process. Calculating a composite index of performance on a set of insight problems may serve a psychometric research agenda, correlating such data with measures of working memory or intelligence, or even personality. Adopting such an individual differences analysis strategy and the data it produces typically implicates working memory or intelligence as playing substantive roles in problem-solving (it would be surprising if it did not), but it doesn't help us understand how a particular problem is solved. A granular coding of the video and audio evidence, as illustrated here, helps us identify the process through which a new idea was discovered. My methodological demonstration used matchstick arithmetic problems (and a small subset of such problems to boot): one, perhaps, worries about the singular nature of these problems and the relatively narrow remit of the exploration, with consequences for generalizing to other types of insight problems. There is, however, good evidence that a first-order procedure employed with different insight problems, such as the seventeen animals (Vallée-Tourangeau et al., 2016), the triangle of coins (Vallée-Tourangeau et al., 2020), the socks problem (Ross & Vallée-Tourangeau, 2021b), and anagram solving (Ross & Vallée-Tourangeau, 2022b) provide rich data that illustrate the critical role played by objects in the discovery of new ideas (constructing physical models of probabilistic reasoning problems also transforms and improves performance; see G. Vallée-Tourangeau et al., 2015).

The data generated in this manner is more qualitative in nature. Achieving the granularity required to capture the role of objects, and to identify other solution processes, is costly. For starters, participants are run individually, but the bulk of the cost of data processing and analysis is in the transcription and subsequent content analysis of these transcriptions. This simple exploratory experiment generated a bank 168 videos, each individually coded using ELAN. I reported a very small proportion of the corpus of utterances that were extracted from these videos. In my opinion, the more critical contribution of the analysis strategy enacted through the ELAN platform is the ability to juxtapose two streams of data. People have hazy hunches or sharper ideas to be sure and can articulate them. In problem-solving, the idea that corresponds to the solution of the problem (e.g., decomposing the plus operator in $I = II + II$) must be discovered. Where and how does this idea come about? As described above, a second-order procedure can only deliver a mental origin explanation. A first-order procedure, wherein people interact with objects, can enact a different explanation for the origin of a new idea. The innovative procedure illustrated here offers a method for linking changes in the participants' internal mental reflections with the external changes in the world, and a coding methodology that enables the precise measure of the timing and nature of both, unveiling the dialogue between a problem solver and things. The procedure generated two streams of data: (i) verbal protocol from the participants and (ii) physical changes to the model of the solution. The originality and significance of the methodological proposal lie in the close consideration of how these two streams of data intersect. Their temporal juxtaposition is particularly informative: how the verbal protocol anticipates the movement of the object, how it reacts to unanticipated results from a change to the object, or yet a third possibility, how thinking and the change in the object are co-determined, reflected in the synchronous evolution between idea development and object transformation. Whereas previous research has mined verbal protocol data for participants' strategies and hypotheses (e.g., Fleck & Weisberg, 2013) none have tried to map the coordination or dialogue between object and thought.

First-Order Procedure Employed by Insight Researchers. It is important to mention that not all insight problem-solving research proceeds with what I call a second-order procedure, namely one where the participants don't interact with objects to construct models of the solution. It remains true, though, that researchers using matchstick arithmetic as a tool to study creative problem-solving primarily adopt a second order rather than a first-order procedure, that is use static displays of the matchsticks (e.g., Bilalić et al., 2021; with few exceptions, e.g., Danek et al., 2016). Still, there are important studies on the 8-coin problem (e.g., Öllinger et al., 2013; Ormerod et al., 2002), the 10-penny problem (Öllinger et al., 2017); the 9-dot problem (e.g., Danek et al., 2016), and the 5-square problem (e.g., Fedor et al., 2015) that explore problem-solving with material artefacts, and participants physically interact with these to create models of the solution (solution prototypes as it were). What is particularly fascinating in these studies (namely, Danek et al., 2016; Fedor et al., 2015; Öllinger et al., 2013; Öllinger et al., 2017; Ormerod et al., 2002), is that while objects are manipulated, the causal inferences that researchers wish to draw about the genesis of a new idea is strictly in terms of mental mechanisms that act on mental representations. In addition, even when in a few instances researchers video record the session (and many don't), the video data are not coded to capture a developmental trajectory of how the model of the solution was shaped through action, and even more important, *none* obtain concurrent verbal protocols as was done in the illustrative experiment reported here. As a result, researchers cannot capture the dialogue between participants and objects as they work together to construct the model of the solution. Researchers express some frustration about the lack of analytic traction offered by concepts such as restructuring and representational change: 'The restructuring hypothesis does not explain the process that generates the candidate hypotheses during conscious search and the process that leads to restructuring' (Fedor et al., 2015, p. 12). But the commitment to a cognitivist explanation remains unwavering even among those researchers who employ an interactive procedure. The main goal of the exploratory experiment reported here is to alert researchers of the inattentional blindness concerning the role of objects as a co-constitutive factor in the genesis of a new idea.

Dialogue with the Experimenter. Let me offer brief reflections on the nature of the verbal protocols recorded in this experiment, as well as the nature of the post-solution interview questions that were posed to better understand the participants' explanation of how they solved the problem. The verbal protocols collected through the minimal dialogue between participants and experimenter are more like what Ericsson and Simon (1998) call a Level 3 type, that is 'socially directed speech' with a present or imaginary interlocutor. Verbal protocols are typically employed to offer a window on the exact cognitive mechanisms responsible for basic mental operations. However, my aim was more modest in some sense: Verbal protocols were collected to help me identify one of three solution processes, namely analytic, outsight, and insight. The resulting protocols may well fit a Level 3 category, and as such may have even mitigated the manifestation of outsight, by encouraging a more analytic way of solving the problem. As Ericsson and Simon (1998, p. 182) write '(. . .) when participants are asked to describe and explain their thinking, their performance is often changed – mostly it is improved'.

The Scarcity of Pure Insight

In this exploratory experiment, matchstick arithmetic problems were generally solved more often and quicker with interactivity than without (see Appendix). Participants in the control condition can solve these problems too and sometimes quickly. It may well be that profiling participants in terms of maths anxiety, working memory, creative self-efficacy (Karwowski et al., 2018) or creative anxiety (Daker et al., 2020) could have offered a clearer window onto how and why some participants were more adroit than others at mentally simulating movements to arrive at a solution. These measures of individual differences might have also helped us better understand how and why interactivity helped some participants more than others, or even how participants engaged with the model of the solution, that is the extent and nature of their interaction with the object-qua-model of the solution. Kirsh (2009, 2010) has written eloquently on the cost structure of cognition: coupling thinking with the manipulation of artefacts incurs a cost, and some participants either undervalue the return on investment or deem the investment too onerous.

The benefit of interactivity was most sharply observed for the second problem, namely I = II + II. According to Knoblich et al. (1999) solving this problem proceeds necessarily from relaxing the operator constraint: participants may naturally focus first on modifying operands in searching for a solution, but for this problem they must appreciate that the operator can be deconstructed, transforming the plus operator into a minus (moving the vertical stick from the plus to the left to create a new operand, and hence the solution, namely I = III − II). Here the quasi-strategic, and at time playful, movement of the sticks in the interactive condition was most helpful, and indeed the rate of outsight was highest for the second problem (75 per cent) than for either the first (39 per cent) or third (48 per cent) problem. Half of the participants in the control condition also solved this problem (compared with 86 per cent in the interactive condition) but it's worth noting that these participants solved it within the first 3 minutes: working on the problem for another 2 minutes did not help the remaining participants (see the cumulative solution curves plotted in Figure A3 in the Appendix). It is also important to note that relaxing the operator constraint is not sufficient to solve this problem. There were instances in the control condition for problem 2 where participants clearly entertained the hypothesis that the solution might involve turning the plus into a minus, but still could not mentally simulate the matchstick movement that would result in the correct configuration. Table 9 reports a particularly illustrative case of a participant in the control condition whose verbal protocol clearly indicated that this constraint was relaxed but who could not discover the solution: Within the first 30 seconds (see the bold entries in the table) the participant entertains the possibility of turning the plus into a minus, but never manages to hold onto the mental image of the minus while simultaneously and systematically mentally simulating the movement of the 'freed' vertical stick. For example, at 31.25 he voices I = II − II, but seems unable to mentally project where the vertical stick from the plus operator might go, as if it has disappeared from his mental workspace. It is plausible to suggest that had he been able to physically change the appearance of the equation by creating a minus, he would have *seen* the freed floating vertical stick, which then might have triggered actions, creating and observing new objects, in his quest for the answer.

In the control condition, participants primarily discovered the solution through an analytic process. Of the fifty-seven solutions recorded in that condition, thirty-five (or 61 per cent) were identified as analytic, while twenty (or 35 per cent) were classified as insight. Thus, as operationalized by our coding criteria, insight accounted for a little over a third of the solutions in the control condition. The classification strategy employed here, though, probably overestimates the rate of a so-called pure insight sequence — that is, protracted impasse followed by sudden illumination along with aha! phenomenology — since the insight classification was also a default category, that is it

Table 9 Transcript from P16 in the control condition working on Problem 2 (I = II + II).

00:02.7	E	Ok I'll start the timer
00:06.1	P	deleting in three, two, one . . . so one equals two plus two, so that would be
00:14.3	P	er, you can't move the line across because that would be two equals one plus two so that wouldn't work, so you would have to, one two three four . . . so we'd have to make that
00:25.0	P	either a one, you can't move the one across because then you've got zero equals two plus three so that wouldn't work
00:31.3	**P**	**if you made that a minus it would become two minus two which would equal zero. so . . . one**
00:42.1	**P**	**you can't do one minus one, two plus, minus one wouldn't work there either so it's got to be . . . moving one across would be one plus two, minus two and it's only moving one again so we**
00:53.8	P	we can't do that, one equals . . . can't turn the equals into a plus because that will be one plus two plus
01:03.1	P	two (inaudible) equals sign would have to be one equals two plus two, can't er . . . one plus three that wouldn't work
01:14.9	P	either, one equals two plus two . . . two that will be two equals one plus two that will give you
01:26.7	**P**	**three . . . make that a minus that would then be one minus two . . . two minus one**
01:41.1	**P**	**and it's only moving one stick correct? ok I was going to say you could move across and make three minus one but that would be moving two so that wouldn't work**
01:44.1	E	yes
01:52.3	P	one equals two plus two . . . two plus two . . . could we move
02:02.5	**P**	**that one away that would then make it so it's one plus two equals two which wouldn't work, if you want to move . . . that would just be two minus two**
02:15.4	P	which would equal zero not equals two so that doesn't work, oh I hate this one Anna, um
02:28.0	P	no because you'd have to move two to do that as well, so that would then be three plus one, that doesn't work
02:40.2	P	three . . . I don't know. God I'm stumped on this one . . . so two
02:51.7	P	two divided by two . . . I'm not sure because that needs to get . . . so you've got the same on both side but moving one from there that still gives you three not two

Table 9 (cont.)

03:03.7	P	but that's not going to work so we then need to do one to that, so that'll be three plus one but that will be four not a one
03:14.1	P	moving the one across will give a zero but then that will give you minus one not the (inaudible) so that wouldn't work . . . if you did two plus
03:27.3	**P**	**two minus one would equal two so that wouldn't work because it couldn't be a minus that would still give you something positive**
03:36.4	P	ohhh god . . . need more coffee. One equals two plus two
03:47.4	**P**	**one stick . . . (whispers) change the plus to a minus that's two sticks**
03:59.5	P	if it's two plus one that will be three which wouldn't work either
04:11.0	P	I don't know (laughs) this one's stumping me and it's kind of annoying
04:17.6	P	er, because I don't see how you can rearrange that because that on that side it would be
04:25.8	P	two on the left and you've still got two positive on the right
04:31.5	P	so you would have to turn that into a negative but then to turn that into a negative
04:37.1	**P**	**two minus two wouldn't give you two, it would give you zero**
04:41.8	P	(inaudible) you're not moving one so that wouldn't matter
04:50.8	**P**	**two minus two no, you can't move that because that would involve moving**
05:02.7	P	two as well in front of the equals(?) that will be one plus two so that wouldn't work
05:10.3	E	time up
05:11.5	P	damn (laughs)

Note: The time stamp in the first column shows minutes:seconds.deciseconds.
P = Participants, E = Experimenter.

was employed for cases that did not clearly meet either analytic or outsight criteria.

A non-interactive or second-order procedure can only perform solution processes that are evinced mentally (and as mentioned above, even researchers employing a first-order procedure don't sufficiently instrumentalize it to capture the dialogue with objects). A second-order procedure authorizes only mental mechanisms that strain working memory resources since the participant must mentally rehearse specific hypotheses, design a strategy to test them, monitor the test outcomes without ever seeing them, all while constructing mental images of possible configurations. All that mental effort is clearly on evidence in the verbal protocols from the non-interactive condition. (Quick and sudden solutions are more difficult to interpret in the verbal protocol data, and they may be the result of putative unconscious processes of the kind proposed by Ohlsson (e.g., 1984, 1992). A second-order procedure is predicated on and promotes a rigid dualist separation of subject – qua participant – and object – qua physical model of the solution: not only are subject and object separate entities, the ontological chiasm is also reinforced by preventing the subject from manipulating the object. The object, in turn, is inert, does nothing, and clearly a solution can only be the product of cognitive processes inherent to the subject. Methodologies are performative, and a second-order procedure performs a mentalist explanation of creative problem-solving.

In the interactive condition, insight accounted for 11 per cent of the solution processes, while analysis for 35 per cent. By far the most common solution process was outsight (54 per cent). An interactive procedure, where participants can interact with and modify a physical model of the solution, encouraged exploration of different models, which in over 50 per cent of the cases resulted in constructing configurations that seeded the solution. A first-order procedure encourages the participants to interact and modify a physical model of the solution. The ontological separation between subject and object is fuzzier here, the boundaries more porous, as evidenced by their concurrent becoming, that is how a participant's knowledge undergoes transformations in step with the transformations of the object. Subject and object are actants in a system of knowledge, their interaction reconfigures that system until it corresponds with the solution to the problem: the knowledge is distributed, just as cognition is. Far from attributing agency to the object, the appearance of the object through its modifications has agentic consequences, not unlike how the behaviour of the ball in rugby has agentic consequences for the players on the pitch. The dynamic properties of the object are a source of knowledge (see Ross & Vallée-Tourangeau's (2021a) kinenoetic analysis). The idea of the correct solution emerges from the participant's engagement with the object. As the procedure employed in the interactive condition demonstrates, outsight is a very common process by which the correct solution is discovered when participants can manipulate the model of the solution. It is through ELAN and the granular coding of the participants' utterances and the changes in the physical appearance and the equally granular juxtaposition of both streams of data that help us capture and see, plainly, the phenomenon of outsight (see Vallée-Tourangeau et al., 2024, for a detailed case study of outsight).

Restructuring

Mental restructuring is a term often employed to describe the process by which an impasse is overcome. Ohlsson (1984) adapted information processing concepts and offered a vocabulary that have guided insight problem-solving research for decades. He offered a 'distinction between the problem and the problem solver's mental representation of it' (p. 119) and defined restructuring as a 'change in the problem solver's mental representation of the problem' (p. 119). There is a trap in this formulation, however: Unless we can independently assess and track the mental representations and the cognitive processes that transform them, stating that a problem is solved because a mental representation has been restructured is just another way of describing the result, rather than explaining it. Ohlsson goes on to describe the cognitive mechanisms that can effect restructuring in terms of semantic memory search and spreading of activation (see his Principle 4, p. 122). When and if the problem solver is stuck, experiences an impasse, their search through a 'description space' with its associated operators, does not bring the goal state within a mental horizon: 'The horizon is as far ahead as the problem solver can "see" in his head' (p. 124, and I note, in passing, the deeply entrenched mentalist perspective: to see *in the head* rather than seeing in the world). Thus, Ohlsson offers an information-processing framework and a theoretical vocabulary of problem and description spaces that are explored as means to evince mental restructuring. As to what triggers search in a description space, Ohlsson postulates a 'meta-heuristic' that is itself triggered when the participant experiences an impasse: the frustrating inability to identify operators that can be applied to the mental representation of a problem cues a 'restructure-when-stuck' (p. 123) heuristic (note incidentally that Fleck & Weisberg's (2013) verbal protocol data revealed that restructuring can take place without impasse). Thus, an impasse engages efforts, conscious or otherwise, to redescribe the problem to yield a more productive mental representation, which in turn would be associated with operators that could transform this representation to bring the solution within the reasoner's mental horizon. Ohlsson illustrates this process with Wertheimer's problem of determining the area of a figure that looks like a parallelogram overlapping a square, until this representation is restructured into overlapping triangles, which then can be mentally rearranged into a more congenial mental representation, by mentally removing the overlap to create the mental representation of a square (see pp. 125–127; note how Ohlsson illustrates this process with a graphical representation of geometrical shapes that afford manipulation).

What draws my attention in Ohlsson's information-processing treatment of mental restructuring, is another meta-heuristic that has been ignored by creative problem-solving researchers, namely, the 'restructure-upon-novelty' (p. 123) heuristic: 'If detailed observation of the problem situation reveals previously unsuspected aspects, it makes sense to try to re-interpret the entire situation in terms of them'. But here novelty is not assumed to be produced by changes in the world, but rather by dissipating something akin to inattentional blindness: Something that was there to 'see' all along was ignored but is now the focus of attention. Outsight is a form of 'restructure-upon-novelty' heuristic, triggered not by an internal attentional process, but rather by the dynamic nature of the physical environment through which thinking takes place. There is plenty of evidence of the 'restructure-when-stuck' efforts in the participants' verbal protocols reported here, abandoning unproductive hypotheses and assumptions, and labouring new perspectives to unlock the solution. What the first-order procedure makes manifest is the 'restructure-upon-novelty'. I would go further here in that outsight is a phenomenon where mental restructuring follows rather than precedes physical restructuring: Outsight is not an attentional process applied to a static physical representation of the problem, but rather the product of a dynamic one wrought through interactivity. Outsight collapses the mental and the physical into a single process of discovery. Through their own playful or quasi-strategic actions, problem solvers produce solution prototypes that cue the next action and that sometimes simply offer the answer.

Having said this, prototyping is not necessary, and indeed is not possible other than through effortful mental simulation, for correctly solving the matchstick problems in the non-interactive condition. Perhaps the notion of prototyping should include solution attempts, whether reified materially or simulated mentally. It behoves researchers to explore in granular details how such attempts play a role in charting the problem-solving trajectory (by the nature of the feedback they provide). That this trajectory remains considerably easier to map on the basis of the material traces left by the dynamic changes to the model of the solution, is a key benefit of adopting a first-order procedure.

Systemic Creative Problem-Solving

Typically, accounts of creative problem-solving are hylomorphic in nature (Ingold, 2010). That is, a change in the object, here the model of the solution, is preceded by a change in an internal mind: the starting assumption of these models is that a solution is physically implemented on the basis of an idea, the causal directionality here goes from mind to matter. Such hylomorphic accounts are simply blind to the phenomenon of outsight. The methodology illustrated here and the theoretical invitation to restore objects in problem-solving map a rigorous, systemic perspective on cognition and creativity. Disciplinary exigencies encourage cognitive psychologists to adopt certain procedures that constrain the nature of the explanation. In creativity research, the explanation is formulated in terms of idea generation, associative abilities, and mental restructuring (see also Weisberg, 2023). Outside the laboratory, physical prototyping is a key to guiding and determining problem-solving activity (see Schrage, 1999). This takes thinking outside of the brain, distributing it across an ensemble of heterogenous elements that configure a cognitive ecosystem (Hutchins, 2010). By integrating experimental and qualitative methods, the programme of research illustrated here aims to better understand simple cognitive ecosystems and how interactivity within these systems gives rise to new ideas. From this post-cognitivist perspective, a human agent qua problem solver comingles with a non-human one, namely the physical model of the proto-solution that morphs into the normative configuration through the action and reaction of the human agent. There is a double process of becoming: the human agent's developmental appreciation of the correct answer co-evolves with the physical transformation of the non-human actant, here the object as a physical model of the problem, morphs into a shape that gradually approximates the normative correct configuration. Therefore, to ignore the behaviour of the non-human object would be to ablate a large chunk from the explanation of the participant's ability to solve the problem: Objects and thoughts *go together*.

Appendix

Experimental Procedure

All participants were tested remotely through Zoom. Participants were sent a link to a short Qualtrics survey where answers for informed consent questions were collected as well as basic demographic questions (gender and age; the informed consent and demographic questions survey as well as the PowerPoint slide deck employed in this experiment can be found on the OSF).[1] The experiment received a favourable opinion from Kingston University's Research Ethics Committee.

Once the survey was completed, the participant was emailed a deck of slides. Each slide, save for the first one, was obscured by a grey screen which could be deleted to reveal the contents underneath. The participant was instructed to launch the PowerPoint application and open the file; at this point, the participant was asked to share their screen and the recording of the session began (and the experimenter turned off their camera). The participant viewed the deck of slides in edit mode.

Participants were given the following instructions, adapted from Perkins (1981; see also Fleck & Weisberg, 2013) in which they are asked to narrate aloud their thoughts and to comments on their actions while they tackle the problems.

> While solving the problems you will be encouraged to think aloud. When thinking aloud you should do the following. Say whatever's on your mind. Don't hold back hunches, guesses, wild ideas, images, plans, or goals. Speak as continuously as possible. Try to say something at least once every five seconds. Speak audibly. Watch for your voice dropping as you become involved. Don't worry about complete sentences or eloquence.
>
> Don't over explain or justify. Analyze no more than you would normally. Don't elaborate on past events. Get into the pattern of saying what you're thinking about now, not of thinking for a while and then describing your thoughts. Though the experimenter is present you are not talking to the experimenter. Instead, you are to perform this task as if you are talking aloud to yourself.

---

[1] The survey also recorded the participant's email contact and this for three reasons: each participant was entitled to a £10 voucher as remuneration, which was sent to them via email; this email address was also a means to identify the participant's data since they were given the opportunity to withdraw their data up to two-weeks post-participation (none did); finally the researcher needed the participant's email address to send them the experimental material at the start of the session. Email addresses were expunged from the data file after the completion of the study.

Participants were then given 3 minutes to practice speaking their thoughts while they engaged in a simple word search puzzle. They used the drawing tools in PowerPoint to select a highlighter with which to trace target words from the letter matrix. The experimenter prompted the participant to articulate their search strategy, where they were looking at or what they were looking for. With the practice session completed, the next phase of the procedure introduced the matchstick arithmetic problems. Participants were told that three simple arithmetic expressions would be presented in turn; each was an incorrect expression in Roman numerals that could be turned into a correct one by moving one matchstick.

Before the first problem was presented, Participants in the interactive condition were trained to move three vertical sticks from the top left corner of the slide into one of three vertical slots in the middle right of the slide (see Figure A1): They did so by selecting/clicking on each of the sticks and dragging it into the target location in turn. As Figure A1 illustrates the work surface for this training exercise, as well as the one employed for each of the three problems, was a 3 × 18 grid: Columns were labelled A through R, and the rows AA to CC. The procedure was thus instrumentalized to facilitate the precise coding of the movement of a stick during the problem-solving task.

With training complete, the three problems were then presented in turn and in the order illustrated in Figure A2: First **II = III + I**, second **I = II + II**, and third **III = II − I**. The first problem is solved by decomposing the III right of the equal sign and moving a matchstick to the II on the left of the equal sign; the second

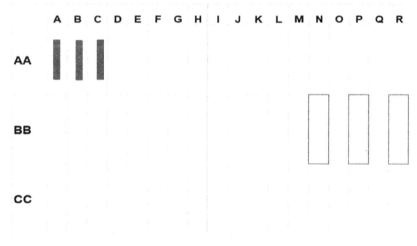

Figure A1 The practice work surface where the participant selected and dragged sticks from their location in the top left corner to each one of the landing rectangles on the right of the surface.

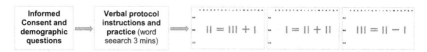

Figure A2 Test procedure, starting with informed consent questions, followed by a verbal protocol training exercise for 3 minutes, and then the presentation of the three matchstick arithmetic problems (the participant allocated up to 5 minutes to solve each problem.

problem is solved by decomposing the plus operator and moving the vertical stick from the operator to the left, adding it to the II; there were two possible solutions for the third problem, either decomposing the equal sign and moving one horizontal stick to the minus operator to create an equal sign (viz., III − II = I) or moving a stick from the III on the left of the equal sign to the II on the right (viz., II = III − I). Participants in the interactive condition were encouraged to move sticks to help the solve the problems and the instructions read 'It's important to move different sticks to try out different configurations or arrangements to discover which single stick in a different location makes a difference'.

Solution Rates and Latencies

Twenty-three participants (or 85 per cent) in the interactive condition and twenty (or 74 per cent) participants in the control condition solved Problem 1 (II = II + I); twenty-four participants (or 86 per cent) in the interactive condition and thirteen participants (or 48 per cent) in the control condition solved Problem 2 (I = II + II); finally, twenty-seven participants (or 100 per cent) in the interactive condition and twenty-four participants (or 89 per cent) in the control conditions solved Problem 3 (III = II − I).

The mean latencies for the three problems in both conditions are shown in Table A1. These were generally lower in the interactive condition than in the control condition. Clearly these means are distorted by the non-solvers (with latencies of 300 seconds; one solver in the Control condition announced the solution at the 300-second mark, P18, Problem 1) of which there were more in the Control condition. To obtain a clearer picture on solution latencies, a survival analysis was conducted (Mantel-Haenszel log-rank; JASP version 0.18.3) on the cumulative solution rates for participants in both conditions and this for each of the three problems (Knoblich et al., 1999, also report cumulative solution rates across time). The 5-minute period allocated for work on each problem was segmented in terms of fifteen 20-second bins, and the cumulative number of participants solving the problem across time bins in both conditions is plotted for each of the three problems in Figure A3. Inspecting the left panel

Table A1 Latencies (Lat. in Seconds) and Solution Processes (SP) for each of the three problems in the interactive and control conditions.

			Interactive									Control					
			II = III + I		I = II + II		III = II − I					II = III + I		I = II + II		III = II − I	
ID	G	Age	Lat.	SP	Lat.	SP	Lat.	SP	ID	G	Age	Lat.	SP	Lat.	SP	Lat.	SP
P3	M	28	46	O-E	300		102	O-E	P4	F	32	127	A	300		37	A
P5	F	29	108	A	31	A	73	O-Ph	P6	M	28	162	I	300		182	A
P7	F	22	61	O-Ph	300		26	A	P8	M	35	38	A	174	A	31	A
P9	F	24	23	O-Ph	243	O-E	22	A	P10	F	28	87	I	300		65	A
P11	F	27	44	A	66	A	60	A	P12	F	24	103	I	300		27	I
P13	M	28	18	O-E	71	O-E	30	O-E	P14	M	28	58	A	300		28	I
P15	M	29	24	A	192	O-E	33	A	P16	M	29	300	I	47	A	40	I
P17	F	29	95	O-E	128	O-E	47	O-Ph	P18	F	29	161	I	93	A	43	A
P19	M	28	300		123	A	78	O-Ph	P20	F	26	125	I	300		19	I
P21	M	29	67	I	250	O-Ph	21	A	P22	F	63	300		300		90	I
P23	F	28	300		29	O-Ph	14	A	P24	M	28			300	I	300	
P25	F	26	12	A	80	O-E	72	O-E	P26	F	28	74	A	54	I	62	I

Table A1 (cont.)

Interactive

ID	G	Age	II = III + I Lat.	SP	I = II + II Lat.	SP	III = II − I Lat.	SP
P27	F	32	47	I	280	O-Ph	80	O-Ph
P29	F	23	130	O-E	258	O-Ph	80	O-Ph
P31	F	58	192	I	204	A	15	A
P33	F	28	21	I	222	O-Ph	14	A
P35	M	29	25	O-Ph	300		69	O-Ph
P37	F	28	300		90	O-Ph	116	O-Ph
P39	F	29	109	A	56	O-E	51	O-E
P41	F	28	50	I	151	O-Ph		
P43	M	29	37	A	140	O-E	12	A
P45	M	28	21	I	197	O-E	18	A
P47	M	25	24	A	122	A	48	A
P49	M	29	300		300		212	I
P51	M	28	79	O-Ph	32	O-E	24	O-E
P53	M	29			193	O-E	22	A

Control

ID	G	Age	II = III + I Lat.	SP	I = II + II Lat.	SP	III = II − I Lat.	SP
P28	F	35	300		296	A	86	A
P30	M	29	206	I	32	A	22	I
P32	M	31	300		46	A	80	A
P34	F	37	133	A	61	A	40	A
P36	F	42	45	I	300		300	
P38	F	25	300		300		300	
P40	F	27	50	A	133	A	204	I
P42	M	28	300		300		46	A
P44	F	28	41	A	300		22	I
P46	F	25	300		232			
P48	F	27	139	A	247	A	120	O-Ph
P50	F	28	62	A	300		176	I
P52	M	29	300		84	A	14	A
P54	M	28	31	A	300		160	O-Ph

P55	M	27	42	O-E	35	A	46	I	P56	F	26	76	I	43	A	19	A
P57	F	28	22	A	134	O-Ph	54		P58	F	28	288	A	175	A	35	A
M		28.8	92.5		161.7		53.3				30.4	163.2		208.0		94.4	
SD		6.1	97.2		93.5		42.9				7.5	106.1		109.6		91.8	

Notes. Exclusions are as follows. P41, Problem 3: The experimenter accidentally told the participant the answer to the problem in resetting the start state midway. P53, Problem 1: The participant hid a stick to create the solution, a move that was unnoticed by the experimenter. P4, Problem 1, the participant moved the sticks to create the solution despite instructions not to do so; P4, Problem 2, the participant created a right to left solution (namely I = II – III) but was not corrected by the experimenter and participant allowed to proceed to the final problem. P46, Problem 2, the participant gave up; P46, Problem 3, the solution slide (at the end of the deck) was accidentally accessed during work on the third problem.

A = Analysis, I = Insight; O-Ph = Post hoc outsight; O-E = Enacted outsight.

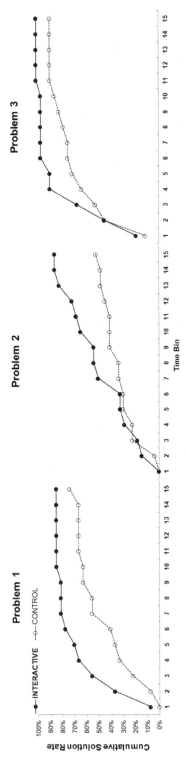

Figure A3 Cumulative solution rate in the interactive (full line, black circles) and control (dashed line, open circles) condition for each of the three problems as a function of time, segmented in fifteen 20-second time bins.

of Figure A3, we note that for the first problem, the cumulative solution rates display a negative exponential curve for the interactive condition where 78 per cent of the participants have solved the problem after 120 seconds (vs. 41 per cent in the control condition); the solution curve shows a steadier linear increase in the control condition; the difference was significant, $\chi^2(1, N = 54) = 4.517$, $p = .034$. The middle panel plots the cumulative solution rates for the second problem. Both curves are more linear, although while the cumulative solution rate in the interactive condition increases linearly throughout the 5-minute session (to reach 86 per cent), it asymptotes slightly above 40 per cent at the 3-minute mark in the control condition; the difference between conditions was significant, $\chi^2(1, N = 55) = 5.688$, $p = .017$. As for Problem 3, the cumulative solution curves are similar in both conditions, but the negative exponential function more pronounced in the interactive condition: the 96 per cent asymptote is reached at the 2-minute mark in the interactive condition, whereas the 89 per cent asymptote is reached by 4-minute mark in the control condition; the difference between conditions was, however, non-significant, $\chi^2(1, N = 54) = 3.554$, $p = .059$.

References

Abraham, A. (2023). Why the standard definition of creativity fails to capture the creative act. *Qeios*, 1–13. https://doi.org/10.32388/LS88G9; https://www.qeios.com/read/LS88G9.

Archibald, M. M., Ambagtsheer, R. C., Casey, M. G., & Lawless, M. (2019). Using Zoom videoconferencing for qualitative data collection: Perceptions and experiences of researchers and participants. *International Journal of Qualitative Methods*, *18*, 1–8. https://doi.org/10.1177/1609406919874596.

Bar-Hillel, M. (2021). Stumpers: An annotated compendium. *Thinking & Reasoning*, *27*(4), 536–566. https://doi.org/10.1080/13546783.2020.1870247.

Benedek, M., & Neubauer, A. C. (2013). Revisiting Mednick's model on creativity-related differences in associative hierarchies: Evidence for a common path to uncommon thought. *The Journal of Creative Behavior*, *47*(4), 273–289. https://doi.org/10.1002/jocb.35.

Bilalić, M., Graf, M., Vaci, N., & Danek, A. H. (2021). The temporal dynamics of insight problem solving–restructuring might not always be sudden. *Thinking & Reasoning*, *27*(1), 1–37. https://doi.org/10.1080/13546783.2019.1705912.

Böhmer, A. I., Sheppard, S., Kayser, L., & Lindemann, U. (2017). Prototyping as a thinking approach in design: Insights of problem-solving activities while designing a product. In *2017 International Conference on Engineering, Technology and Innovation (ICE/ITMC)*, pp. 955–963. https://doi.org/10.1109/ICE.2017.8279985.

Bowden, E. M., & Grunewald, K. (2018). Whose insight is it anyway? In F. Vallée-Tourangeau (Ed.), *Insight: On the origins of new ideas* (pp. 28–50). Routledge.

Bryant, L. (1976). The development of the diesel engine. *Technology and Culture*, *17*(3), 432–446. https://doi.org/10.2307/3103523.

Buchman, L. M. (2021). *Make to know: From space of uncertainty to creative discovery*. Thames & Hudson.

Carson, S. H., Peterson, J. B., & Higgins, D. M. (2003). Decreased latent inhibition is associated with increased creative achievement in high-functioning individuals. *Journal of Personality and Social Psychology*, *85*(3), 499–506. https://doi.org/10.1037/0022-3514.85.3.499.

Chuderski, A., & Jastrzębski, J. (2018). Much ado about aha!: Insight problem solving is strongly related to working memory capacity and reasoning ability. *Journal of Experimental Psychology: General*, *147*(2), 257–281. https://doi.org/10.1037/xge0000378.

Clark, A. (1997). *Being there: Putting brain, body, and world together again.* MIT Press.

Coulter, J. (1991). Cognition: Cognition in an ethnomethodological mode. In G. Button (Ed.), *Ethnomethodology and the human sciences* (pp. 176–195). Cambridge University Press.

Csikszentmihalyi, M. (2014). *The systems model of creativity: The collected works of Mihaly Csikszentmihalyi.* Springer.

Daker, R. J., Cortes, R. A., Lyons, I. M., & Green, A. E. (2020). Creativity anxiety: Evidence for anxiety that is specific to creative thinking, from STEM to the arts. *Journal of Experimental Psychology: General, 149*(1), 42–57. https://doi.org/10.1037/xge0000630.

Danek, A. H. (2023). The phenomenology of insight: The Aha experience. In L. J. Ball, & F. Vallée-Tourangeau (Eds.), *The Routledge international handbook of creative cognition* (pp. 308–331). Routledge.

Danek, A. H., Wiley, J., & Öllinger, M. (2016). Solving classical insight problems without Aha! experience: 9 dot, 8 coin, and matchstick arithmetic problems. *The Journal of Problem Solving, 9*(1), 47–57. https://doi.org/10.7771/1932-6246.1183.

Darwin, C. (1958). *The autobiography of Charles Darwin 1809-1882. With the original omissions restored. Edited and with appendix and notes by his grand-daughter Nora Barlow.* Collins.

Duncker, K. (1945). On problem-solving. *Psychological Monographs, 58*(5), i–113. https://doi.org/10.1037/h0093599.

Ericsson, K. A., & Simon, H. A. (1998). How to study thinking in everyday life: Contrasting think-aloud protocols with descriptions and explanations of thinking. *Mind, Culture, and Activity, 5*(3), 178–186. https://doi.org/10.1207/s15327884mca0503_3.

Fedor, A., Szathmáry, E., & Öllinger, M. (2015). Problem solving stages in the five square problem. *Frontiers in Psychology, 6*(1050). https://doi.org/10.3389/fpsyg.2015.01050; https://www.frontiersin.org/journals/psychology/articles/10.3389/fpsyg.2015.01050/full.

Fleck, J. I., & Weisberg, R. W. (2013). Insight versus analysis: Evidence for diverse methods in problem solving. *Journal of Cognitive Psychology, 25*(4), 436–463. https://doi.org/10.1080/20445911.2013.779248.

Gilhooly, K. J. (2019). *Incubation in problem solving and creativity: Unconscious processes.* Routledge.

Gilhooly, K. J., & Fioratou, E. (2009). Executive functions in insight versus non-insight problem solving: An individual differences approach. *Thinking & Reasoning, 15*(4), 355–376. https://doi.org/10.1080/13546780903178615.

Gilhooly, K. J., Georgiou, G., & Devery, U. (2013). Incubation and creativity: Do something different. *Thinking & Reasoning, 19*(2), 137–149. https://doi.org/10.1080/13546783.2012.749812.

Gilhooly, K. J., & Webb, M. E. (2018). Working memory in insight problem solving. In F. Vallée-Tourangeau (Ed.), *Insight: On the origins of new ideas* (pp. 105–119). Routledge.

Gruber, H. E., & Barrett, P. H. (1974). *Darwin on man: A psychological study of creativity.* Wildwood House.

Hartmann, B., Klemmer, S. R., Bernstein, M., et al. (2006). Reflective physical prototyping through integrated design, test, and analysis. In *Proceedings of the 19th annual ACM Symposium on User Interface Software and Technology* (pp. 299–308). https://doi.org/10.1145/1166253.1166300.

Hutchins, E. (2010). Cognitive ecology. *Topics in Cognitive Science, 2*, 705–715. https://doi.org/10.1111/j.1756-8765.2010.01089.x.

Ingold, T. (2010). The textility of making. *Cambridge Journal of Economics, 34*, 91–102. https://doi.org/10.1093/cje/bep042.

JASP Team (2024). JASP (Version 0.18.3) [Computer software]. https://jasp-stats.org/faq/how-do-i-cite-jasp/.

Karwowski, M., Lebuda, I., & Wiśniewska, E. (2018). Measuring creative self-efficacy and creative personal identity. *International Journal of Creativity & Problem Solving, 28*(1), 45–57.

Kimmel, M., & Groth, C. (2024). What affords being creative? Opportunities for novelty in light of perception, embodied activity, and imaginative skill. *Adaptive Behavior, 32*(3) 225–242. https://doi:10.1177/10597123231179488.

Kirsh, D. (2009). Projection, problem space and anchoring. In N. A. Taatgen, & H. van Rijn (Eds.), *Proceedings of the Thirty-First Annual Conference of the Cognitive Science Society* (pp. 2310–2315). Cognitive Science Society.

Kirsh, D. (2010). Thinking with external representations. *AI & Society, 25*, 441–454. https://doi.org/10.1007/s00146-010-0272-8.

Knoblich, G., Ohlsson, S., Haider, H., & Rhenius, D. (1999). Constraint relaxation and chunk decomposition in insight problem solving. *Journal of Experimental Psychology: Learning, Memory, and Cognition, 25*(6), 1534–1555. https://doi.org/10.1037/0278-7393.25.6.1534.

Kocienda, K. (2018). *Creative selection: Inside Apple's design process during the golden age of Steve Jobs.* St Martin's Press.

Köhler, W. (1925). *The mentality of apes.* Kegan Paul, Trench, Trubner.

Latour, B. (1987). *Science in action: How to follow scientists and engineers through society.* Harvard University Press.

Latour, B. (1988). *The pasteurization of France.* Harvard University Press.

Latour, B. (1999). *Pandora's hope.* Harvard University Press.

Latour, B. (2005). *Reassembling the social*. Oxford University Press.

Latour, B. (2013). *An inquiry into modes of existence: An anthropology of the moderns*. Harvard University Press.

Latour, B., & Woolgar, S. (1986). *Laboratory life: The construction of scientific facts*. Princeton University Press.

Law, J. (2004). *After method: Mess in social science research*. Routledge.

Li, Y., Beaty, R. E., Luchini, S., et al. (2023). Accelerating creativity: Effects of transcranial direct current stimulation on the temporal dynamics of divergent thinking. *Creativity Research Journal, 35*(2), 169–188. https://doi.org/10.1080/10400419.2022.2068297.

Lynch, M., & Woolgar, S. (1990). *Representation in scientific practice*. MIT Press.

Malafouris, L. (2020). Thinking as 'thinging': Psychology with things. *Current Directions in Psychological Science, 29*(1), 3–8. https://doi.org/10.1177/0963721419873349.

March, P. L. (2024). *Clayful phenomenology and material engagement: Explorations in contemporary cognitive archaeology*. DPhil dissertation, Department of Archaeology, Keble College, Oxford. https://img-cache.oppcdn.com/fixed/49156/assets/SXvW6Yz2cdMKUqbJ.pdf.

March, P. L., & Malafouris, L. (2023). Art through material engagement . . . and vice versa. In L. J. Ball, & F. Vallée-Tourangeau (Eds.), *Routledge international handbook of creative cognition* (pp. 585–604). Routledge.

Mednick, S. A. (1962). The associative basis of the creative process. *Psychological Review, 69*, 220–232. https://doi.org/10.1037/h0048850.

Ohlsson, S. (1984). Restructuring revisited II: An information processing theory of restructuring and insight. *Scandinavian Journal of Psychology, 25*, 117–129. https://doi.org/10.1111/j.1467-9450.1984.tb01005.x.

Ohlsson, S. (1992). Information-processing explanations of insight and related phenomena. In M. T. Keane, & K. J. Gilhooly (Eds.), *Advances in the psychology of thinking* (Vol. 1, pp. 1–44). Harvester-Wheatsheaf.

Öllinger, M., Fedor, A., Brodt, S., & Szathmáry, E. (2017). Insight into the ten-penny problem: Guiding search by constraints and maximization. *Psychological Research, 81*(5), 925–938. https://doi.org/10.1007/s00426-016-0800-3.

Öllinger, M., Jones, G., Faber, A. H., & Knoblich, G. (2013). Cognitive mechanisms of insight: The role of heuristics and representational change in solving the eight-coin problem. *Journal of Experimental Psychology: Learning, Memory, and Cognition, 39*(3), 931–939. https://doi.org/10.1037/a0029194.

Ormerod, T. C., MacGregor, J. N., & Chronicle, E. P. (2002). Dynamics and constraints in insight problem solving. *Journal of Experimental Psychology: Learning, Memory, and Cognition, 28*(4), 791–799. https://doi.org/10.1037//0278-7393.28.4.791.

Oswick, C., & Robertson, M. (2009). Boundary objects reconsidered: From bridges and anchors to barricades and mazes. *Journal of Change Management, 9*(2), 179–193. https://doi.org/10.1080/14697010902879137.

Perkins, D. N. (1981). *The mind's best work*. Harvard University Press.

Ross, W., & Vallée-Tourangeau, F. (2021a). Kinenoetic analysis: Unveiling the material traces of insight. *Methods in Psychology, 5*, 100069. https://doi.org/10.1016/j.metip.2021.100069.

Ross, W., & Vallée-Tourangeau, F. (2021b). Rewilding cognition: Complex dynamics in open experimental systems. *Journal of Trial and Error, 2*(1), 30–39. https://doi.org/10.36850/e4.

Ross, W., & Vallée-Tourangeau, F. (2022a). Insight with stumpers: Normative solution data for 25 stumpers and a fresh perspective on the accuracy effect. *Thinking Skills and Creativity, 46*, 101114. https://doi.org/10.1016/j.tsc.2022.101114.

Ross, W., & Vallée-Tourangeau, F. (2022b). Accident and agency: A mixed methods study contrasting luck and interactivity in problem solving. *Thinking & Reasoning, 28*(4), 487–528. https://doi.org/10.1080/13546783.2021.1965025.

Schön, D. A. (1982). *The reflective practitioner: How professionals think in action*. Basic Books.

Schön, D. A., & Bennett, J. (1996). Reflective conversation with materials. In T. Winograd (Ed.), *Bringing design to software* (pp. 171–184). ACM Press.

Schrage, M. (1999). *Serious play: How the world's best companies simulate to innovate*. Harvard Business School Press.

Serres, M. (1994). *Éclaircissements: Entretiens avec Bruno Latour*. Flammarion.

Star, S. L., & Griesemer, J. R. (1989). Institutional ecology, 'translations' and boundary objects: Amateurs and professionals in Berkeley's Museum of Vertebrate Zoology, 1907–39. *Social Studies of Science, 19*(3), 387–420. https://doi.org/10.1177/030631289019003001.

Steffensen, S. V., Vallée-Tourangeau, F., & Vallée-Tourangeau, G. (2016). Cognitive events in a problem-solving task: Qualitative methods for investigating interactivity in the 17 animals problem. *Journal of Cognitive Psychology, 28*, 79–105. https://doi.org/10.1080/20445911.2015.1095193.

Toon, A. (2011). Playing with molecules. *Studies in History and Philosophy of Science Part A, 42*(4), 580–589. https://doi.org/10.1016/j.shpsa.2011.08.002.

Trasmundi, S. B., & Steffensen, S. V. (2024). Dialogical cognition. *Language Sciences, 103*, 101615. https://doi.org/10.1016/j.langsci.2024.101615.

Vallée-Tourangeau, F. (2023a). Insight in the kinenoetic field. In L. J. Ball, & F. Vallée-Tourangeau (Eds.), *Routledge international handbook of creative cognition* (pp. 127–139). Routledge. https://doi.org/10.4324/9781003009351.

Vallée-Tourangeau, F. (2023b). *Systemic creative cognition: Bruno Latour for creativity researchers*. Routledge.

Vallée-Tourangeau, F., & March, P. L. (2020). Insight out: Making creativity visible. *Journal of Creative Behavior, 54*(4), 824–842. https://doi.org/10.1002/jocb.409.

Vallée-Tourangeau, F., Ross, W., Ruffato Rech, R., & Vallée-Tourangeau, G. (2020). Insight as discovery. *Journal of Cognitive Psychology, 33*(6–7), 718–737. https://doi.org/10.1080/20445911.2020.1822367.

Vallée-Tourangeau, F., Steffensen, S. V., Vallée-Tourangeau, G., & Sirota, M. (2016). Insight with hands and things. *Acta Psychologica, 170*, 195–205. https://doi.org/10.1016/j.actpsy.2016.08.006.

Vallée-Tourangeau, G., Abadie, M., & Vallée-Tourangeau, F. (2015). Interactivity fosters Bayesian reasoning without instruction. *Journal of Experimental Psychology: General, 144*(3), 581–603. https://doi.org/10.1037/a0039161.

Vallée-Tourangeau, F., Green, A., March, P. L., & Steffensen, S. V. (2024). Object as knowledge: A case study of outsight. *Possibility Studies and Society*. https://doi.org/10.1177/27538699241256021.

Vandevelde, A., Van Dierdonck, R., & Clarysse, B. (2002). *The role of physical prototyping in the product development process*. Vlerick Business School Working Paper. http://hdl.handle.net/20.500.12127/711.

Vygotsky, L. (1934/2012). *Thought and language*, edited and translated by E. Hanfmann, G. Vakar, & A. Kozulin. MIT Press.

Wallas, G. (1926). *The art of thought*. Jonathan Cape.

Watson, J. (1968). *The double helix*. Penguin.

Weisberg, R. W. (1995). Prolegomena to theories of insight in problem solving: A taxonomy of problems. In R. J. Sternberg, & J. E. Davidson (Eds.), *The nature of insight* (pp. 157–196). MIT Press.

Weisberg, R. W. (2015). On the usefulness of 'value' in the definition of creativity. *Creativity Research Journal, 27*, 111–124. https://doi.org/10.1080/10400419.2015.1030320.

Weisberg, R. W. (2023). A quandary in the study of creativity: Conflicting findings from case studies versus the laboratory. In L. Ball & F. Vallee-Tourangeau (Eds.), *Routledge international handbook of creative cognition* (pp. 765–793). Routledge.

Weller, A., Villejoubert, G., & Vallée-Tourangeau, F. (2011). Interactive insight problem solving. *Thinking & Reasoning, 17*, 429–439. https://doi.org/10.1080/13546783.2011.629081.

Wiley, J., & Danek, A. H. (2024). Restructuring processes and Aha! experiences in insight problem solving. *Nature Reviews Psychology*, *3*, 42–55. https://doi.org/10.1038/s44159-023-00257-x.

Wittenburg, P., Brugman, H., Russel, A., Klassmann, A., & Sloetjes, H. (2006). ELAN: A professional framework for multimodality research. In *Proceedings of LREC 2006, Fifth International Conference on Language Resources and Evaluation*. www.lrec-conf.org/proceedings/lrec2006/pdf/153_pdf.pdf.

Zabelina, D., Saporta, A., & Beeman, M. (2016). Flexible or leaky attention in creative people? Distinct patterns of attention for different types of creative thinking. *Memory & Cognition*, *44*, 488–498. https://doi.org/10.3758/s13421-015-0569-4.

Zoom Video Communications Inc. (2016). https://zoom.us/.

Acknowledgements

I would like to thank Susan Cooper, Anna Green, Alicja Perdion, Renata Ruffato Rech, and Eleanor Stocker for their contribution to the research summarized here; Christina Soderberg for her contribution to the revised version of this manuscript (as well as archiving material on the OSF), Paul March with whom some of the ideas presented here were developed (as well as for his editorial suggestions on a previous version of this manuscript), and finally to two anonymous reviewers for their thoughtful comments. Financial support from Kingston University's Faculty of Business and Social Sciences is gratefully acknowledged; Christina Soderberg is supported through a Leverhulme research project grant (RPG-2023–278).

https://orcid.org/0000-0002-9554-5294

Cambridge Elements

Creativity and Imagination

Anna Abraham

University of Georgia, USA

Anna Abraham, Ph.D. is the E. Paul Torrance Professor at the University of Georgia, USA. Her educational and professional training has been within the disciplines of psychology and neuroscience, and she has worked across a diverse range of academic departments and institutions the world over, all of which have informed her cross-cultural and multidisciplinary focus. She has penned numerous publications including the 2018 book, *The Neuroscience of Creativity* (Cambridge University Press), and 2020 edited volume, *The Cambridge Handbook of the Imagination*. Her latest book is *The Creative Brain: Myths and Truths* (2024, MIT Press).

About the Series

Cambridge Elements in Creativity and Imagination publishes original perspectives and insightful reviews of empirical research, methods, theories, or applications in the vast fields of creativity and the imagination. The series is particularly focused on showcasing novel, necessary and neglected perspectives.

Cambridge Elements ≡

Creativity and Imagination

Printed in the United States
by Baker & Taylor Publisher Services